William Shakespeare

Macbeth

HERITAGE CLASSICS

William Shakespeare

Macbeth

HERITAGE

HERITAGE PUBLISHERS

NEW DELHI

HERITAGE PUBLISHERS
19-A, Ansari Road, Daryaganj, New Delhi-110002
Tel.: 23266258, 23264444
Fax: 23263050, E-mail: heritage@nda.vsnl.net.in

ISBN : 9788170262381

Printed in India
Sagar Printers, 23 Ansari Road
New Delhi-110002

About the Author

DETAILS about William Shakespeare's life are sketchy, mostly mere surmise based upon court or other clerical records. His parents, John and Mary (Arden), were married about 1557; she was of the landed gentry, he a yeoman—a glover and commodities merchant. By 1568, John had risen through the ranks of town government and held the position of high bailiff, similar to mayor. William, the eldest son, was born in 1564, probably on April 23, several days before his baptism on April 26, 1564. That Shakespeare also died on April 23, 52 years later, may have resulted in the adoption of this birthdate.

William no doubt attended the local grammar school in Stratford where his parents lived, and would have studied primarily Latin rhetoric, logic, and literature. At age 18 (1582), William married Anne Hathaway, a local farmer's daughter eight years his senior. Their first daughter, Susanna, was born six months later (1583), and twins Judith and Hamnet were born in 1585.

Shakespeare's life can be divided into three periods: the first 20 years in Stratford, which include his schooling, early marriage, and fatherhood; the next 25 years as an actor and playwright in London; and the last five in retirement back in Stratford where he enjoyed moderate wealth gained from his theatrical successes. The years linking the first two periods are marked by a lack of information about Shakespeare, and are often referred to as the "dark years"; the transition from active work into retirement was gradual and cannot be precisely dated.

John Shakespeare had suffered financial reverses from William's teen years until well into the height of the playwright's popularity and success. In 1596, John Shakespeare was granted a coat of arms, almost certainly purchased by William, who the next year bought a sizable house in Stratford. By the time of his death, William had substantial properties, both professional and personal, which he bestowed on his theatrical associates and his family (primarily his daughter Susanna, having rewritten his will one month before his death to protect his assets from Judith's new husband, Thomas Quiney, who ran afoul of church doctrine and public esteem before and after the marriage).

Shakespeare probably left school at 15, which was the norm, and took some sort of job, especially since this was the period of his father's financial difficulty. Numerous references in his plays suggest that William may have in fact worked for his father, thereby gaining specialized knowledge.

At some point during the "dark years," Shakespeare began his career with a London theatrical company—perhaps in 1589—for he was already an actor and playwright of some note in 1592. Shakespeare apparently wrote and acted for Pembroke's Men, as well as numerous others, in particular Strange's Men, which later became the Chamberlain's Men, with whom he remained for the rest of his career.

When, in 1592, the Plague closed the theaters for about two years, Shakespeare turned to writing book-length narrative poetry. Most notable were "Venus and Adonis" and "The Rape of Lucrece," both of which were dedicated to the Earl of Southampton, whom scholars accept as Shakespeare's friend and benefactor despite a lack of documentation. During the same period, Shakespeare was writing his sonnets, which are more likely signs of the time's fashion rather than actual love poems detailing any particular relationship. He returned to play writing when theaters reopened in 1594, and published no more poetry. His sonnets were published without his consent in 1609, shortly before his retirement.

Amid all of his success, Shakespeare suffered the loss of his only son, Hamnet, who died in 1596 at the age of 11. But Shakespeare's career continued unabated, and in London in 1599, he became one of the partners in the new Globe Theater, built by the Chamberlain's Men. This group was a remarkable assemblage of excellent actors who were also business partners and close personal friends . . . including Richard Burbage who all worked together as equals . . . .

When Queen Elizabeth died in 1603 and was succeeded by her cousin King James of Scotland, the Chamberlain's Men was renamed the King's Men, and Shakespeare's productivity and popularity continued uninterrupted. He invested in London real estate and, one year away from retirement, purchased a second theater, the Blackfriars Gatehouse, in partnership with his fellow actors. His final play was *Henry VIII*, two years before his death in 1616.

Incredibly, most of Shakespeare's plays had never been published in anything except pamphlet form, and were simply extant as acting scripts stored at the Globe. Only the efforts of two of Shakespeare's company, John Heminges and Henry Condell, preserved his 36 plays (minus *Pericles*, the thirty-seventh) in the First Folio. Heminges and Condell published the plays, they said, "only to keep the memory of so worthy a friend and fellow alive as was our Shakespeare". Theater scripts were not regarded as literary works of art, but only the basis for the performance. Plays were a popular form of entertainment for all layers of society in Shakespeare's time, which perhaps explains why Hamlet feels compelled to instruct the traveling Players on the fine points of acting, urging them not "to split the ears of the groundlings," nor "speak no more than is set down for them."

Present copies of Shakespeare's plays have, in some cases, been reconstructed in part from scripts written down by various members of an acting company who performed particular roles. Shakespeare's plays, like those of many of the actors who also were playwrights, belonged to the acting company. The performance, rather than the script, was what concerned the author, for that was how his play would become popular—and how the company, in which many actors were shareholders, would make money.

William Shakespeare died on April 23, 1616, and was buried two days later in the chancel of Holy Trinity Church where he had been baptized exactly 52 years earlier.

Plot Summary

The Play begins with the brief appearance of a trio of witches and then moves to a military camp, where the Scottish King Duncan hears the news that his generals, Macbeth and Banquo, have defeated two separate invading armies—one from Ireland, led by the rebel Macdonald, and one from Norway. Following their pitched battle with these enemy forces, Macbeth and Banquo encounter the witches as they cross a moor. The witches prophesy that Macbeth will be made Thane (a rank of Scottish nobility) of Cawdor and eventually king of Scotland. They also prophesy that Macbeth's companion, Banquo, will beget a line of Scottish kings, although Banquo will never be king himself. The witches vanish, and Macbeth and Banquo treat their prophecies skeptically until some of King Duncan's men come to thank the two generals for their victories in battle and to tell Macbeth that he has indeed been named Thane of Cawdor.

Lady Macbeth desires the kingship for him and wants him to murder Duncan in order to obtain it. He and Lady Macbeth plan to get Duncan's two chamberlains drunk so they will black out. While Duncan is asleep, Macbeth stabs him, despite his doubts and a number of supernatural portents, including a vision of a bloody dagger. When Duncan's death is discovered the next morning, Macbeth kills the chamberlains—ostensibly out of rage at their crime—and easily assumes the kingship. Duncan's sons Malcolm and Donalbain flee to England and Ireland respectively.

Fearful of the witches' prophesy that Banquo's heirs will seize the throne, Macbeth hires a group of murderers to kill Banquo and his son Fleance. They ambush Banquo on his way to a royal feast, but they fail to kill Fleance, who escapes into the night. At the feast that night, Banquo's ghost visits Macbeth. When he sees the ghost, Macbeth raves fearfully, startling his guests, who include most of the great Scottish nobility. Lady Macbeth tries to neutralize the damage, but Macbeth's kingship incites increasing resistance from his nobles and subjects. Frightened, Macbeth goes to visit the witches in their cavern. There, they show him a sequence of demons and spirits who present him with further prophecies.

When news of his family's execution reaches Macduff in England, he is stricken with grief and vows revenge. Prince Malcolm, Duncan's son, has succeeded in raising an army in England, and Macduff joins him as he rides to Scotland to challenge Macbeth's forces. Lady Macbeth, meanwhile, becomes plagued with fits of sleepwalking in which she bemoans what she believes to be bloodstains on her hands. Before Macbeth's opponents arrive, Macbeth receives news that she has killed herself, causing him to sink into a deep and pessimistic despair. Nevertheless, he awaits the English and fortifies Dunsinane, to which he seems to have withdrawn in order to defend himself, certain that the witches' prophecies guarantee his invincibility.

In the battle, Macbeth hews violently, but the English forces gradually overwhelm his army and castle. On the battlefield, Macbeth encounters the vengeful Macduff, who declares that he was not "of woman born" but was instead "untimely ripped" from his mother's womb (what we now call birth by cesarean section). Though he realizes that he is doomed, Macbeth continues to fight until Macduff kills and beheads him. Malcolm, now the king of Scotland, declares his benevolent intentions for the country and invites all to see him crowned at Scone.

The Actors' Names

DUNCAN, King of Scotland

MALCOLM DONALBAIN	his son
MACBETH MANQUO	generals of the King's army
MACDUFF LENNOX ROSS MENTEITH ANGUS CAITHNESS	noblemen of Scotland

FLEANCE, son to Banquo

SIWARD, Earl of Nothumberland, general of the English forces

Young SIWARD, his son

SEYTON, an officer attending on Macbeth

Boy, son to Macduff

An English Doctor

A Scottish Doctor

A Captain

A Soldier

A Porter

An Old Man

Three murderers

LADY MACBETH

LADY MACDUFF
Gentlewoman attending on Lady Macbeth
HECAT
Three Witches
Apparitions
Lords, Gentlemen, Officers, Soldiers, Attendants, and Messengers.

I. 1

A desert place. Thunder and lightning. Enter three Witches.

FIRST WITCH: When shall we three meet again?
In thunder, lightning, or in rain?
SECOND WITCH: When the hurlyburly's done,
When the battle's lost and won.
THIRD WITCH: That will be ere the set of sun.
FIRST WITCH: Where the place?
SECOND WITCH: Upon the Heath.
THIRD WITCH: There to meet with Macbeth.
FIRST WITCH: I come, Graymalkin.
ALL: Paddock calls. Anon!
Fair is foul, and foul is fair.
Hover through the fog and filthy air.

Exeunt.

I. 2

Alarum within. Enter King Duncan, Malcolm, Donalbain, Lennox, with Attendants, meeting a bleeding Captain.

DUNCAN: What bloody man is that? He can report,
As seemeth by his plight, of the revolt
The newest state.
MALCOLM: This is the Sergeant,

Who like a good and hardy soldier fought
'Gainst my captivity. Hail, brave friend!,
Say to the King the knowledge of the broil
As thou didst leave it.

CAPTAIN: Doubtful it stood,
As two spent swimmers that do cling together
And choke their art. The merciless Macdonwald,
(Worthy to be a rebel, for to that
The multiplying villainies of Nature
Do swarm upon him) from the Western Isles
Of kerns and gallowglasses is supplied;
And Fortune, on his damned quarrel smiling,
Show'd like a rebel's whore. But all's too weak;
For brave Macbeth (well he deserves that name)
Disdaining Fortune, with his brandish'd steel,
Which smoked with bloody execution,
(Like Valor's minion) carved out his passage
Till he faced the slave,
Which ne'er shook hands, nor bade farewell to him,
Till he unseam'd him from the nave to the chaps,
And fix'd his head upon our battlements.

DUNCAN: O valiant cousin! Worthy gentleman!

CAPTAIN: As whence the sun 'gins his reflection,
Shipwrecking storms and direful thunders break,
So from that spring whence comfort seem'd to come
Discomfort swells. Mark, King of Scotland, mark.

No sooner justice had, with valour arm'd,
Compell'd these skipping kerns to trust their heels,
But the Norweyan Lord, surveying vantage,
With furbish'd arms and new supplies of men,
Began a fresh assault.

DUNCAN: Dismay'd not this our captains, Macbeth and Banquo.?

CAPTAIN: Yes,
As sparrows eagles, or the hare the lion.
If I say sooth, I must report they were
As cannons overcharged with double cracks,
So they doubly redoubled strokes upon the foe.
Except they meant to bathe in reeking wounds,
Or memorize another Golgotha,
I cannot tell;
But I am faint; my gashes cry for help.

DUNCAN: So well thy words become thee as thy wounds;
They smack of honor both. Go get him surgeons.

Enter Ross and Angus

Who comes here?

MALCOLM: The worthy Thane of Ross.

LENNOX: What a haste looks through his eyes!
So should he look
That seems to speak things strange.

ROSS: God save the King!

DUNCAN: Whence camest thou, worthy Thane?

ROSS: From Fife, great King,
Where the Norweyan banners flout the sky,
And fan our people cold.
Norway himself, with terrible numbers,
Assisted by that most disloyal traitor,
The Thane of Cawdor, began a dismal conflict,
Till that Bellona's bridegroom, lapp'd in proof,
Confronted him with self-comparisons,
Point against point, rebellious arm 'gainst arm,
Curbing his lavish spirit; and, to conclude,
The victory fell on us.
DUNCAN: Great happiness!
ROSS: That now, Sweno, the Norways' king,
Craves composition;
Nor would we deign him burial of his men
Till he disbursed, at Saint Colme's Inch,
Ten thousand dollars, to our general use.
DUNCAN: No more that Thane of Cawdor shall deceive
Our bosom interest. Go pronounce his present death,
And with his former title greet Macbeth.
ROSS: I'll see it done.
DUNCAN: What he hath lost, noble Macbeth hath won.

Exeunt.

I. 3

Thunder, Enter the three Witches

FIRST WITCH: Where hast thou been, sister?
SECOND WITCH: Killing swine
THIRD WITCH: Sister where thou?
FIRST WITCH: A sailor's wife had chestnuts in her lap,
Ans mounch'd, and mounch'd, and mounch'd:
Give me, quoth I.
Aroint thee, witch, the rump-fed ronyon cries.
Her husband's to Aleppo gone, Master o' th' *Tiger:*
But in a sieve I'll thither sail,
And like a rat without at tail,
I'll do, I'll do, and I'll do.
SECOND WITCH: I'll give thee a wind.
FIRST WITCH: Th' art kind.
THIRD WITCH: And I another.
FIRST WITCH: I myself have all the other,
And the very ports they below,
All the quarters that they know,
I' th' shipman's card.
I'll drain him dry as hay:
Sleep shall neither night nor day
Hang upon his penthouse lid;
He shall live a man forbid:
Weary sev'nnights, nine times nine,
Shall he dwindle, peak, and pine;

Though his bark cannot be lost,
Yet it shall be tempest-toss'd.
Look what I have.

SECOND WITCH: Show me, show me.

FIRST WITCH: Here I have a pilot's thumb,
Wreck'd as homeward he did come.

Drum within.

THIRD WITCH: A drum, a drum!
Macbeth doth come.

ALL: The weird sisters, hand in hand,
Posters of the sea and land,
Thus do go, about, about,
Thrice to thine, and thrice to mine,
And thrice again, to make up nine.
Peace! The charm's wound up.

Enter Macbeth and Banquo.

MACBETH: So foul and fair a day I have not seen.

BANQUO: How far is't call'd to Forres? What are these
So wither'd and so wild in their attire,
That look not like the inhabitants o' the earth,
And yet are on't? Live you? or are you aught
That man may question? You seem to understand me,
By each at once her choppy finger laying
Upon her skinny lips. You should be women,
And yet your beards forbid me to interpret
That you are so.

MACBETH: Speak, if you can. What are you?

FIRST WITCH: All hail, Macbeth, hail to thee, Thane of Glamis!

SECOND WITCH: All hail, Macbeth, hail to thee, Thane of Cawdor!

THIRD WITCH: All hail, Macbeth, that shalt be King hereafter!

BANQUO: Good sir, why do you start, and seem to fear
Things that do sound so fair? I' the name of truth,
Are ye fantastical or that indeed
Which outwardly ye show? My noble partner
You greet with present grace and great prediction
Of noble having and of royal hope,
That he seems rapt withal. To me you speak not.
If you can look into the seeds of Time,
And say which grain will grow and which will not,
Speak then to me, who neither beg, nor fear
Your favours, nor your hate.

FIRST WITCH: Hail!

SECOND WITCH. Hail!

THIRD WITCH: Hail!

FIRST WITCH: Lesser than Macbeth, and greater.

SECOND WITCH: Not so happy, yet much happier.

THIRD WITCH: Thou shalt get kings, though thou be none.
So all hail, Macbeth and Banquo!

FIRST WITCH: Banquo and Macbeth, all hail!

MACBETH: Stay, you imperfect speakers, tell me more.
By Sinel's death, I know I am Thane of Glamis;
But how of Cawdor? The Thane of Cawdor lives,
A prosperous gentleman; and to be King
Stands not within the prospect of belief,
No more than to be Cawdor. Say from whence
You owe this strange intelligence, or why
Upon this blasted Heath you stop our way
With such prophetic greeting? Speak, I charge you.

Witches vanish.

BANQUO: The earth hath bubbles, as the water has,
And these are of them. Whither are they vanish'd?
MACBETH: Into the air, and what seem'd corporal,
Melted, as breath into the wind.
Would they had stay'd!
BANQUO: Were such things here as we do speak about?
Or have we eaten on the insane root,
That takes the reason prisoner?
MACBETH: Your children shall be kings.
BANQUO: You shall be King.
MACBETH: And Thane of Cawdor too. Went it not so?
BANQUO: To the selfsame tune and words. Who's here?

Enter Ross and Angus.

ROSS: The King hath happily received, Macbeth,
The news of thy success; and when he reads
Thy personal venture in the rebels' fight,

His wonders and his praises do contend
Which should be thine or his. Silenced with that,
In viewing o'er the rest o' the selfsame day,
He finds thee in the stout Norweyan ranks,
Nothing afeard of what thyself didst make,
Strange images of death. As thick as tale
Came post with post, and every one did bear
Thy praises in his kingdom's great defense,
And pour'd them down before him.

ANGUS: We are sent
To give thee, from our Royal Master thanks;
Only to herald thee into his sight,
Not pay thee.

ROSS: And for an earnest of a greater honour,
He bade me, from him, call thee Thane of Cawdor.
In which addition, hail most worthy Thane,
For it is thine.

BANQUO: What, can the devil speak true?

MACBETH: The Thane of Cawdor lives.
Why do you dress me in borrow'd robes?

ANGUS: Who was the Thane lives yet,
But under heavy judgement bears that life
Which he deserves to lose.
Whether he was combined
With those of Norway, or did line the rebel
With hidden help and vantage, or that with both

He labor'd in his country's wreck, I know not;
But treasons capital, confess'd and proved,
Have overthrown him.

MACBETH: Glamis, and Thane of Cawdor!
The greatest is behind. Thanks for your pains.
Do you not hope your children shall be kings,
When those that gave the Thane of Cawdor to me,
Promised no less to them?

BANQUO: That, trusted home,
Might yet enkindle you unto the Crown,
Besides the Thane of Cawdor. But 'tis strange;
And oftentimes, to win us to our harm,
The instruments of darkness tell us truths,
Win us with honest trifles, to betray's
In deepest consequence.
Cousins, a word, I pray you.

MACBETH: Two truths are told,
As happy prologues to the swelling act
Of the imperial theme; I thank you, gentlemen.
This supernatural soliciting
Cannot be ill, cannot be good. If ill,
Why hath it given me earnest of success,
Commencing in a truth? I am Thane of Cawdor.
If good, why do I yield to that suggestion,
Whose horrid image doth unfix my hair
And make my seated heart knock at my ribs,

Against the use of nature? Present fears
Are less than horrible imaginings:
My thought, whose murther yet is but fantastical,
Shakes so my single state of man that function
Is smother'd in surmise, and nothing is
But what is not.

BANQUO: Look, how our partner's rapt.

MACBETH: If chance will have me King,
Why, chance may crown me,
Without my stir.

BANQUO: New honours come upon him,
Like our strange garments, cleave not to their mould
But with the aid of use.

MACBETH: Come, what come may,
Time and the hour, runs through the roughest day.

BANQUO: Worthy Macbeth, we stay upon your leisure.

MACBETH: Give me your favour; my dull brain was wrought with things forgotten.
Kind gentlemen, your pains are register'd
Where every day I turn the leaf,
To read them.
Let us toward the King.
Think upon what hath chanced, and at more time,
The interim having weigh'd it, let us speak
Our free hearts each to other.

BANQUO: Very gladly.

MACBETH: Till then, enough. Come, friends.

Exeunt.

I. 4

Flourish. Enter King Duncan, Lennox, Malcolm, Donalbain, and Attendants.

DUNCAN: Is execution done on Cawdor?
Are not those in commission yet return'd?
MALCOLM: My Liege, they are not yet come back.
But I have spoke with one that saw him die,
Who did report that very frankly he
Confess'd his treasons,
Implored your Highness' pardon, and set forth
A deep repentance. Nothing in his life became him
Like the leaving it; he died
As one that had been studied in his death,
To throw away the dearest thing he owed
As 'twere a careless trifle.
DUNCAN: There's no art,
To find the mind's construction in the face:
He was a gentleman on whom I built
An absolute trust.

Enter Macbeth, Banquo, Ross, and Angus.

O worthiest cousin!
The sin of my ingratitude even now
Was heavy on me. Thou art so far before,

That swiftest wing of recompense is slow
To overtake thee. Would thou hadst less deserved,
That the proportion both of thanks and payment,
Might have been mine! Only I have left to say,
More is thy due, than more than all can pay.
MACBETH: The service and the loyalty I owe,
In doing it, pays itself.
Your Highness' part is to receive our duties,
And our duties are to your throne and state,
Children and servants, which do but what they should,
By doing everything safe toward your love and honour.
DUNCAN: Welcome hither.
I have begun to plant thee, and will labour
To make thee full of growing. Noble Banquo,
That hast no less deserved, nor must be known
No less to have done so; let me enfold thee,
And hold thee to my heart.
BANQUO: There if I grow,
The harvest is your own.
DUNCAN: My plenteous joys,
Wanton in fullness, seek to hide themselves
In drops of sorrow. Sons, Kinsmen, Thanes,
And you whose places are the nearest, know
We will establish our estate upon
Our eldest, Malcolm, whom we name hereafter,

The Prince of Cumberland; which honour must
Not unaccompanied, invest him only,
But signs of nobleness, like stars, shall shine
On all deservers. From hence to Inverness,
And bind us further to you.

MACBETH: The rest is labour, which is not used for you.
I'll be myself the harbinger, and make joyful
The hearing of my wife, with your approach;
So humbly take my leave.

DUNCAN: My worthy Cawdor!

MACBETH: The Prince of Cumberland: that is a step
On which I must fall down, or else o'erleap,
For in my way it lies. Stars, hide your fires;
Let not light see my black and deep desires.
The eye wink at the hand; yet let that be,
Which the eye fears, when it is done to see.

Exit.

DUNCAN: True, worthy Banquo! He is full so valiant,
And in his commendations I am fed;
It is a banquet to me. Let's after him,
Whose care is gone before to bid us welcome:
It is a peerless kinsman.

Flourish. Exeunt.

I. 5

Enter Lady Macbeth, reading a letter.

LADY MACBETH: *They met me in the day of success, and I have learned by the perfectest report they have more in them than mortal knowledge. When I burnt in desire to question them further, they made themselves air, into which they vanished. Whiles I stood rapt in the wonder of it, came missives from the King, who all-hailed me 'Thane of Cawdor'; by which title, before, these weird sisters saluted me and referred me to the coming on of time with 'Hail, King that shalt be!' This have I thought good to deliver thee, my dearest partner of greatness, that thou mightst not lose the dues of rejoicing, by being ignorant of what greatness is promised thee. Lay it to thy heart, and farewell."*

Glamis thou art, and Cawdor, and shalt be
What thou art promised. Yet do I fear thy nature.
It is too full o' th' milk of human kindness
To catch the nearest way. Thou wouldst be great;
Art not without ambition, but without
The illness should attend it. What thou wouldst highly,
That wouldst thou holily; wouldst not play false,
And yet wouldst wrongly win.
Thou'ldst have, great Glamis,
That which cries, "Thus thou must do, if thou have it;
And that which rather thou dost fear to do,
Than wishest should be undone." Hie thee hither,
That I may pour my spirits in thine ear,

And chastise with the valour of my tongue
All that impedes thee from the golden round,
Which fate and metaphysical aid doth seem
To have thee crown'd withal.

Enter a Messenger.

What is your tidings?

MESSENGER: The King comes here tonight.

LADY MACBETH: Thou'rt mad to say it!
Is not thy master with him? who, were't so,
Would have inform'd for preparation.

MESSENGER: So please you, it is true; our Thane is coming.
One of my fellows had the speed of him,
Who, almost dead for breath, had scarcely more
Than would make up his message.

LADY MACBETH: Give him tending;
He brings great news.

Exit Messenger.

The raven himself is hoarse
That croaks the fatal entrance of Duncan
Under my battlements. Come, you spirits,
That tend on mortal thoughts, unsex me here
And fill me from the crown to the toe, top-full
Of direst cruelty! Make thick my blood,
Stop up the access and passage to remorse,
That no compunctious visitings of Nature

Shake my fell purpose nor keep peace between
The effect and it! Come to my woman's breasts,
And take my milk for gall, your murthering ministers,
Wherever in your sightless substances
You wait on Nature's mischief! Come, thick night,
And pall thee in the dunnest smoke of Hell
That my keen knife see not the wound it makes,
Nor Heaven peep through the blanket of the dark
To cry, "Hold, hold!"

Enter Macbeth.

Great Glamis! Worthy Cawdor!
Greater than both, by the all-hail hereafter!
Thy letters have transported me beyond
This ignorant present, and I feel now
The future in the instant.

MACBETH: My dearest love,
Duncan comes here tonight.

LADY MACBETH: And when goes hence?

MACBETH: Tomorrow, as he purposes.

LADY MACBETH: O, never
Shall sun that morrow see!
Your face, my Thane, is as a book where men
May read strange matters. To beguile the time,
Look like the time; bear welcome in your eye,
Your hand, your tongue; look like the innocent flower,
But be the serpent under it. He that's coming
Must be provided for; and you shall put

This night's great business into my dispatch,
Which shall to all our nights and days to come
Give solely sovereign sway and masterdom.

MACBETH: We will speak further.

LADY MACBETH: Only look up clear;
To alter favour ever is to fear.
Leave all the rest to me.

Exeunt.

I. 6

Oboes and torches.

Enter Duncan, Malcolm, Donalbain, Banquo, Lennox, Macduff, Ross, Angus, and Attendants.

DUNCAN: This castle hath a pleasant seat;
The air nimbly and sweetly recommends itself
Unto our gentle senses.

BANQUO: This guest of summer,
The temple-haunting martlet, does approve,
By his loved mansionry that the Heaven's breath
Smells wooingly here. No jutty, frieze,
Buttress, nor coign of vantage, but this bird
Hath made his pendant bed and procreant cradle;
Where they most breed and haunt, I have observed
The air is delicate.

Enter Lady Macbeth.

DUNCAN: See, see, our honour'd hostess!
The love that follows us sometime is our trouble,

Which still we thank as love. Herein I teach you
How you shall bid God 'ild us for your pains,
And thank us for your trouble.

LADY MACBETH: All our service
In every point twice done, and then done double,
Were poor and single business to contend
Against those honours deep and broad wherewith
Your Majesty loads our house,
For those of old, and the late dignities
Heap'd up to them, we rest your hermits.

DUNCAN: Where's the Thane of Cawdor?
We coursed him at the heels and had a purpose
To be his purveyor; but he rides well,
And his great love, sharp as his spur, hath holp him
To his home before us. Fair and noble hostess,
We are your guest tonight.

LADY MACBETH: Your servants ever,
Have theirs, themselves, and what is theirs, in compt,
To make their audit at your Highness' pleasure,
Still to return your own.

DUNCAN: Give me your hand;
Conduct me to mine host. We love him highly,
And shall continue our graces towards him.
By your leave, hostess.

Exeunt.

I. 7

Obes. Torches. Enter a Sewer and divers Servants with dishes and service, over the stage. Then enter Macbeth.

MACBETH: If it were done when 'tis done, then 'twere well
It were done quickly. If th' assassination
Could trammel up the consequence, and catch,
With his surcease, success; that but this blow
Might be the be-all and the end-all. Here,
But here, upon this bank and school of time,
We'ld jump the life to come. But in these cases
We still have judgement here, that we but teach
Bloody instructions, which being taught return
To plague the inventor. This even-handed justice
Commends the ingredients of our poison'd chalice
To our own lips. He's here in double trust:
First, as I am his kinsman and his subject,
Strong both against the deed; then, as his host,
Who should against his murtherer shut the door,
Not bear the knife myself. Besides, this Duncan
Hath borne his faculties so meek, hath been
So clear in his great office, that his virtues
Will plead like angels trumpet-tongued against
The deep damnation of his taking-off,
And pity, like a naked new-born babe,
Striding the blast, or Heaven's cherubin horsed
Upon the sightless couriers of the air,

Shall blow the horrid deed in every eye,
That tears shall drown the wind. I have no spur
To prick the sides of my intent, but only
Vaulting ambition, which o'erleaps itself
And falls on the other.

Enter Lady Macbeth.

How now, what news?

LADY MACBETH: He has almost supp'd. Why have you left the chamber?

MACBETH: Hath he ask'd for me?

LADY MACBETH: Know you not, he has?

MACBETH: We will proceed no further in this business:
He hath honor'd me of late, and I have bought
Golden opinions from all sorts of people,
Which would be worn now in their newest gloss,
Not cast aside so soon.

LADY MACBETH: Was the hope drunk
Wherein you dress'd yourself? Hath it slept since?
And wakes it now, to look so green and pale
At what it did so freely? From this time,
Such I account thy love. Art thou afeard
To be the same in thine own act and valour
As thou art in desire? Wouldst thou have that
Which thou esteem'st the ornament of life
And live a coward in thine own esteem,
Letting "I dare not" wait upon "I would"

Like the poor cat i' th' adage?
MACBETH: Prithee, peace!
I dare do all that may become a man;
Who dares do more is none.
LADY MACBETH: What beast was't then
That made you break this enterprise to me?
When you durst do it, then you were a man,
And, to be more than what you were, you would
Be so much more the man. Nor time nor place
Did then adhere, and yet you would make both.
They have made themselves, and that their fitness now
Does unmake you. I have given suck and know
How tender 'tis to love the babe that milks me:
I would, while it was smiling in my face,
Have pluck'd my nipple from his boneless gums
And dash'd the brains out, had I so sworn
As you have done to this.
MACBETH: If we should fail?
LADY MACBETH: We fail?
But screw your courage to the sticking-place,
And we'll not fail. When Duncan is asleep;
(Whereto the rather shall his day's hard journey
Soundly invite him) his two chamberlains
Will I with wine and wassail so convince
That memory, the warder of the brain,
Shall be a fume and the receipt of reason

A limbeck only. When in swinish sleep,
Their drenched natures lie as in a death,
What cannot you and I perform upon
Th' unguarded Duncan? What not put upon
His spongy officers, who shall bear the guilt
Of our great quell?

MACBETH: Bring forth men-children only,
For thy undaunted mettle should compose
Nothing but males. Will it not be received,
When we have mark'd with blood those sleepy two
Of his own chamber and used their very daggers,
That they have done 't?

LADY MACBETH: Who dares receive it other,
As we shall make our griefs and clamour roar
Upon his death?

MACBETH: I am settled and bend up
Each corporal agent to this terrible feat.
Away, and mock the time with fairest show:
False face must hide what the false heart doth know.

Exeunt.

II. 1

Enter Banquo and Fleance, bearing a torch before him.

BANQUO: How goes the night, boy?

FLEANCE: The moon is down; I have not heard the clock.

BANQUO: And she goes down at twelve.

FLEANCE: I take't 'tis later, sir.
BANQUO: Hold, take my sword.
There's husbandry in heaven,
Their candles are all out. Take thee that too.
A heavy summons lies like lead upon me,
And yet I would not sleep. Merciful powers,
Restrain in me the cursed thoughts that nature
Gives way to in repose!

Enter Macbeth and a Servant with a torch.

Give me my sword. Who's there?
MACBETH: A friend.
BANQUO: What, sir, not yet at rest? The King's a-bed.
He hath been in unusual pleasure
Ans sent forth great largess to your offices.
This diamond he greets your wife withal,
By the name of most kind hostess,
And shut up in measureless content.
MACBETH: Being unprepared,
Our will became the servant to defect,
Which else should free have wrought.
BANQUO: All's well.
I dreamt last night of the three weird sisters:
To you they have show'd some truth.
MACBETH: I think not of them;
Yet, when we can entreat an hour to serve,
We would spend it in some words upon that business,

If you would grant the time.

BANQUO: At your kind'st leisure.

MACBETH: If you shall cleave to my consent, when 'tis,
It shall make honour for you.

BANQUO: So I lose none
In seeking to augment it, but still keep
My bosom franchised and allegiance clear,
I shall be counsel'd.

MACBETH: Good repose the while.

BANQUO: Thanks, sir, the like to you.

Exeunt Banquo. and Fleance.

MACBETH: Go bid thy Mistress, when my drink is ready,
She strike upon the bell. Get thee to bed.

Exit Servant.

Is this a dagger, which I see before me,
The handle toward my hand? Come, let me clutch thee.
I have thee not, and yet I see thee still.
Art thou not, fatal vision, sensible
To feeling as to sight? Or art thou but
A dagger of the mind, a false creation,
Proceeding from the heat-oppressed brain?
I see thee yet, in form as palpable
As this which now I draw.
Thou marshal'st me the way that I was going,
And such an instrument I was to use.
Mine eyes are made the fools o' th' other senses,

Or else worth all the rest. I see thee still,
And on thy blade and dudgeon, gouts of blood,
Which was not so before. There's no such thing:
It is the bloody business which informs
Thus to mine eyes. Now o'er the one half-world
Nature seems dead, and wicked dreams abuse
The curtain'd sleep; witchcraft celebrates
Pale Hecat's offerings; and wither'd Murther,
Alarum'd by his sentinel, the wolf,
Whose howl's his watch, thus with his stealthy pace,
With Tarquin's ravishing strides, towards his design
Moves like a ghost. Thou sure and firm-set earth,
Hear not my steps, which way they walk, for fear
Thy very stones prate of my whereabout,
And take the present horror from the time,
Which now suits with it. Whiles I threat, he lives;
Words to the heat of deeds too cold breath gives.

A bell rings.

I go, and it is done; the bell invites me.
Hear it not, Duncan, for it is a knell
That summons thee to Heaven, or to Hell.

Exit.

II. 2

Enter Lady Macbeth.

LADY MACBETH: That which hath made them drunk hath made me bold;
What hath quench'd them hath given me fire.
Hark, Peace! It was the owl that shriek'd,
The fatal bellman, which gives the stern'st good night.
He is about it: the doors are open,
And the surfeited grooms do mock their charge
With snores. I have drugg'd their possets
That death and nature do contend about them,
Whether they live or die.

MACBETH: Who's there' what, ho!

LADY MACBETH: Alack, I am afraid they have awaked
And 'tis not done. The attempt and not the deed
Confounds us. Hark! I laid their daggers ready;
He could not miss 'em. Had he not resembled
My father as he slept, I had done't.
Enter Macbeth,
My husband!

MACBETH: I have done the deed.
Didst thou not hear a noise?

LADY MACBETH: I heard the owl scream and the crickets cry.
Did not you speak?

MACBETH: When?

LADY MACBETH: Now.

MACBETH: As I descended?

LADY MACBETH: Ay.

MACBETH: Hark!
Who lies i' the second chamber?

LADY MACBETH: Donalbain.

MACBETH: This is a sorry sight.

LADY MACBETH: A foolish thought, to say a sorry sight.

MACBETH: There's one did laugh in's sleep,
And one cried,
"Murther!"
That they did wake each other. I stood and heard them,
But they did say their prayers and address'd them
Again to sleep.

LADY MACBETH: There are two lodged together.

MACBETH: One cried, "God bless us!" and "Amen" the other,
As they had seen me with these hangman's hands.
Listening their fear, I could not say "Amen,"
When they did say, "God bless us!"

LADY MACBETH: Consider it not so deeply.

MACBETH: But wherefore could not I pronounce "Amen"?
I had most need of blessing, and "Amen"
Stuck in my throat.

LADY MACBETH: These deeds must not be thought
After these ways; so, it will make us mad.

MACBETH: I heard a voice cry, "Sleep no more!
Macbeth does murther sleep," the innocent sleep,

Sleep that knits up the ravel'd sleave of care,
The death of each day's life, sore labor's bath,
Balm of hurt minds, great Nature's second course,
Chief nourisher in life's feast.

LADY MACBETH: What do you mean?

MACBETH: Still it cried, "Sleep no more!" to all the House;
"Glamis hath murther'd sleep, and therefore Cawdor
Shall sleep no more. Macbeth shall sleep no more."

LADY MACBETH: Who was it that thus cried? Why, worthy Thane,
You do unbend your noble strength, to think
So brainsickly of things. Go, get some water
And wash this filthy witness from your hand.
Why did you bring these daggers from the place?
They must lie there. Go carry them, and smear
The sleepy grooms with blood.

MACBETH: I'll go no more.
I am afraid to think what I have done;
Look on't again I dare not.

LADY MACBETH: Infirm of purpose!
Give me the daggers. The sleeping and the dead
Are but as pictures; 'tis the eye of childhood
That fears a painted devil. If he do bleed,
I'll gild the faces of the grooms withal,
For it must seem their guilt.

Exit. Knock within.

MACBETH: Whence is that knocking?
How is't with me, when every noise appals me?
What hands are here? Ha, they pluck out mine eyes!
Will all great Neptune's ocean wash this blood
Clean from my hand? No, this my hand will rather
The multitudinous seas incarnadine,
Making the green one, red.

Re-enter Lady Macbeth.

LADY MACBETH: My hands are of your colour, but I shame
To wear a heart so white.

Knock

I hear knocking at the south entry.
Retire we to our chamber.
A little water clears us of this deed.
How easy is it then! Your constancy
Hath left you unattended.

Knock

Hark, more knocking.
Get on your nightgown, lest occasion call us,
And show us to be watchers. Be not lost
So poorly in your thoughts.
MACBETH: To know my deed, 'twere best not know myself.

Knocking

Wake Duncan with thy knocking!
I would thou couldst!

Exeunt.

II. 3

Enter a Porter. Knocking within.

PORTER: Here's a knocking indeed! If a man were Porter of Hell Gate, he should have old turning the key. *(Knock)*. Knock, knock, knock! Who's there, i' the name of Belzebub? Here's a farmer that hanged himself on th' expectation of plenty. Come in time! Have napkins enow about you; here you'll sweat fort' *(Knock)*. Knock, knock! Who's there, in th' other Devil's name? Faith, here's an equivocator that could swear in both the scales against either scale, who committed treason enough for God's sake, yet could not equivocate to Heaven. O, come in, equivocator. *(Knock)*. Knock, knock, knock! Who's there? Faith, here's an English tailor come hither, for stealing out of a French hose. Come in, tailor; here you may roast your goose. *(Knock)*. Knock, knock! Never at quiet! What are you? But this place is too cold for Hell. I'll devil-porter it no further. I had thought to have let in some of all professions, that go the primrose way to th' everlasting bonfire. *(Knock)*. Anon, anon! I pray you, remember the porter. Opens the gate.

Enter Macduff and Lennox.

MACDUFF: Was it so late, friend, ere you went to bed,
That you do lie so late?

PORTER: 'Faith, sir, we were carousing till the second cock; and drink, sir, is a great provoker of three things.

MACDUFF: What three things does drink especially provoke?

PORTER: Marry, sir, nose-painting, sleep, and urine. Lechery, sir, it provokes and unprovokes: it provokes the desire, but it takes away the performance. Therefore much drink may be said to be an equivocator with lechery: it makes him, and it mars him; it sets him on, and it takes him off; it persuades him and disheartens him; makes him stand to and not stand to; in conclusion, equivocates him in a sleep, and giving him the lie, leaves him.

MACDUFF: I believe drink gave thee the lie last night.

PORTER: That it did, sir, i' the very throat on me; but requited him for his lie, and, I think, being too strong for him, though he took up my legs sometime, yet I made shift to cast him.

Enter Macbeth.

MACDUFF: Is thy master stirring?
Our knocking has awaked him; here he comes.

LENNOX: Good morrow, noble sir.

MACBETH: Good morrow, both.

MACDUFF: Is the King stirring, worthy Thane?

MACBETH: Not yet.

MACDUFF: He did command me to call timely on him;
I have almost slipp'd the hour.

MACBETH: I'll bring you to him.

MACDUFF: I know this is a joyful trouble to you,
But yet 'tis one.

MACBETH: The labour we delight in physics pain.
This is the door.
MACDUFF: I'll make so bold to call,
For 'tis my limited service.

Exit.

LENNOX: Goes the King hence today?
MACBETH: He does; he did appoint so.
LENNOX: The night has been unruly.
Where we lay, our chimneys were blown down,
And, as they say, lamentings heard i' the air,
Strange screams of death,
And prophesying with accents terrible
Of dire combustion and confused events
New hatch'd to the woeful time.
The obscure bird clamor'd the livelong night.
Some say the earth was feverous
And did shake.
MACBETH: 'Twas a rough night.
LENNOX: My young remembrance cannot parallel
A fellow to it.

Re-enter Macduff.

MACDUFF: O horror, horror, horror! Tongue nor heart
Cannot conceive nor name thee.
MACBETH and LENNOX. What's the matter?
MACDUFF: Confusion now hath made his masterpiece.
Most sacrilegious murther hath broke ope.

The Lord's anointed temple and stole thence
The life o' the building.

MACBETH: What is't you say, the life?

LENNOX: Mean you his Majesty?

MACDUFF: Approach the chamber, and destroy your sight
With a new Gorgon. Do not bid me speak;
See, and then speak yourselves. Awake, awake!

Exeunt Macbeth and Lennox.

Ring the alarum bell. Murther and treason!
Banquo and Donalbain! Malcolm, awake!
Shake off this downy sleep, death's counterfeit,
And look on death itself! Up, up, and see
The great doom's image! Malcolm! Banquo!
As from your graves rise up, and walk like sprites
To countenance this horror! Ring the bell.

Bell rings.

Enter Lady Macbeth.

LADY MACBETH: What's the business,
That such a hideous trumpet calls to parley
The sleepers of the house? Speak, speak!

MACDUFF: O gentle Lady,
'Tis not for you to hear what I can speak:
The repetition in a woman's ear
Would murther as it fell.

Enter Banquo.

O Banquo, Banquo!

Our Royal Master's murther'd.

LADY MACBETH: Woe, alas!
What, in our house?

BANQUO: Too cruel anywhere.
Dear Duff, I prithee, contradict thyself,
And say it is not so.

Enter Macbeth and Lennox with Ross.

MACBETH: Had I but died an hour before this chance,
I had lived a blessed time, for from this instant
There's nothing serious in mortality.
All is but toys; renown and grace is dead,
The wine of life is drawn, and the mere lees
Is left this vault to brag of.

Enter Malcolm and Donalbain.

DONALBAIN: What is amiss?

MACBETH: You are, and do not know't.
The spring, the head, the fountain of your blood
Is stopped, the very source of it is stopp'd.

MACDUFF: Your Royal father's murther'd.

MALCOLM: O, by whom?

LENNOX: Those of his chamber, as it seem'd, had done't.
Their hands and faces were all badged with blood;
So were their daggers, which unwiped, we found
Upon their pillows.
They stared, and were distracted;
No man's life was to be trusted with them.

MACBETH: O, yet I do repent me of my fury,
That I did kill them.

MACDUFF: Wherefore did you so?

MACBETH: Who can be wise, amazed, temperate and furious,
Loyal and neutral, in a moment? No man.
The expedition of my violent love
Outrun the pauser' reason. Here lay Duncan,
His silver skin laced with his golden blood,
And his gash'd stabs look'd like a breach in Nature
For Ruin's wasteful entrance; there, the murtherers,
Steep'd in the colors of their trade, their daggers
Unmannerly breech'd with gore. Who could refrain,
That had a heart to love, and in that heart
Courage to make 's love known?

LADY MACBETH: Help me hence, hoa!

MACDUFF: Look to the lady.

MALCOLM: Why do we hold our tongues,
That most may claim this argument for ours?

DONALBAIN: What should be spoken here,
Where our fate, hid in an auger hole,
May rush and seize us?
Let's away,
Our tears are not yet brew'd.

MALCOLM: Nor our strong sorrow
Upon the foot of motion.

BANQUO: Look to the lady.
And when we have our naked frailties hid,
That suffer in exposure, let us meet
And question this most bloody piece of work
To know it further. Fears and scruples shake us.
In the great hand of God I stand, and thence
Against the undivulged pretense, I fight
Of treasonous malice.
MACDUFF: And so do I.
ALL: So all.
MACBETH: Let's briefly put on manly readiness,
And meet i' th' Hall together.
ALL: Well contented.

Exeunt

MALCOLM: What will you do?
Let's not consort with them.
To show an unfelt sorrow is an office
Which the false man does easy.
I'll to England.
DONALBAIN: To Ireland, I;
Our separated fortune shall keep us both the safer.
Where we are there's daggers in men's smiles;
The near in blood, the nearer bloody.
MALCOLM: This murtherous shaft that's shot
Hath not yet lighted, and our safest way
Is to avoid the aim. Therefore to horse;

And let us not be dainty of leave-taking,
But shift away. There's warrant in that theft
Which steals itself when there's no mercy left.

Exeunt.

II. 4

Enter Ross with an Old Man.

OLD MAN: Three score and ten I can remember well,
Within the volume of which time I have seen
Hours dreadful and things strange, but this sore night
Hath trifled former knowings.
ROSS: Ha, good father,
Thou seest the Heavens, as troubled with man's act,
Threatens his bloody stage. By th' clock 'tis day,
And yet dark night strangles the travelling lamp.
Is't night's predominance, or the day's shame,
That darkness does the face of earth entomb,
When living light should kiss it?
OLD MAN: 'Tis unnatural,
Even like the deed that's done. On Tuesday last
A falcon towering in her pride of place
Was by a mousing owl hawk'd at and kill'd.
ROSS: And Duncan's horses (a thing most strange and certain)
Beauteous and swift, the minions of their race,
Turn'd wild in nature, broke their stalls, flung out,

Contending 'gainst obedience, as they would
Make war with mankind.

OLD MAN: 'Tis said they eat each other.

ROSS: They did so, to the amazement of mine eyes
That look'd upon't.

Enter Macduff.

Here comes the good Macduff.
How goes the world, sir, now?

MACDUFF: Why, see you not?

ROSS: Is't known who did this more than bloody deed?

MACDUFF: Those that Macbeth hath slain.

ROSS: Alas, the day!
What good could they pretend?

MACDUFF: They were suborn'd:
Malcolm and Donalbain, the King's two sons,
Are stol'n away and fled, which puts upon them
Suspicion of the deed.

ROSS: 'Gainst nature still!
Thriftless ambition, that wilt ravin up
Thine own life's means! Then 'tis most like
The sovereignty will fall upon Macbeth.

MACDUFF: He is already named, and gone to Scone
To be invested.

ROSS: Where is Duncan's body?

MACDUFF: Carried to Colmekill,
The sacred storehouse of his predecessors
And guardian of their bones.

ROSS: Will you to Scone?
MACDUFF: No, cousin, I'll to Fife.
ROSS: Well, I will thither.
MACDUFF: Well, may you see things well done there.
Adieu,
Lest our old robes sit easier than our new!
ROSS: Farewell, father.
OLD MAN: God's benison go with you and with those
That would make good of bad and friends of foes!

Exeunt omness

III. 1

Enter Banquo.

BANQUO: Thou hast it now: King, Cawdor, Glamis, all,
As the weird women promised, and I fear
Thou play'dst most foully for't; yet it was said
It should not stand in thy posterity,
But that myself should be the root and father
Of many kings. If there come truth from them
As upon thee, Macbeth, their speeches shine
Why, by the verities on thee made good,
May they not be my oracles as well
And set me up in hope? But hush, no more.

Sennet sounds. Enter Macbeth as King, Lady Macbeth as Queen, Lennox, Ross, Lords, Ladies, and Attendants.

MACBETH: Here's our chief guest.

LADY MACBETH: If he had been forgotten,
It had been as a gap in our great feast
And all-thing unbecoming.
MACBETH: Tonight we hold a solemn supper, sir,
And I'll request your presence.
BANQUO: Let your Highness
Command upon me, to the which my duties
Are with a most indissoluble tie
Forever knit.
MACBETH: Ride you this afternoon?
BANQUO: Ay, my good lord.
MACBETH: We should have else desired your good advice,
Which still hath been both grave and prosperous
In this day's council; but we'll take tomorrow.
Is't far you ride'!
BANQUO: As far, my Lord, as will fill up the time
'Twixt this and supper. Go not my horse the better,
I must become a borrower of the night
For a dark hour or twain.
MACBETH: Fail not our feast.
BANQUO: My Lord, I will not.
MACBETH: We hear our bloody cousins are bestow'd
In England and in Ireland, not confessing
Their cruel patricide, filling their hearers
With strange invention. But of that tomorrow,
When therewithal we shall have cause of state

Craving us jointly. Hie you to horse; adieu,
Till you return at night. Goes Fleance with you?

BANQUO: Ay, my good Lord. Our time does call upon 's.

MACBETH: I wish your horses swift and sure of foot,
And so I do commend you to their backs.
Farewell.

Exit Banquo.

Let every man be master of his time
Till seven at night; to make society
The sweeter welcome, we will keep ourself
Till supper time alone. While then, God be with you!

Exeunt all but Macbeth and a Servant.

Sirrah, a word with you. Attend those men
Our pleasure?

ATTENDANT: They are, my Lord, without the palace gate.

MACBETH: Bring them before us.

Exit Servant.

To be thus is nothing, but to be safely thus.
Our fears in Banquo. Stick deep,
And in his royalty of nature
Reigns that which would be fear'd. 'Tis much he dares,
And, to that dauntless temper of his mind,
He hath a wisdom that doth guide his valour
To act in safety. There is none but he
Whose being I do fear; and under him

My genius is rebuked, as it is said
Mark Antony's was by Caesar. He chid the sisters
When first they put the name of King upon me,
And bade them speak to him; then prophet-like
They hail'd him father to a line of kings.
Upon my head they placed a fruitless crown
And put a barren sceptre in my gripe,
Thence to be wrench'd with an unlineal hand,
No son of mine succeeding. If't be so,
For Banquo's issue have I filed my mind,
For them the gracious Duncan have I murther'd,
Put rancors in the vessel of my peace
Only for them, and mine eternal jewel
Given to the common enemy of man,
To make them kings, the seed of Banquo Kings!
Rather than so, come, Fate, into the list,
And champion me to the utterance! Who's there?

Enter Servant with two Murtherers.

Now go to the door, and stay there till we call.

Exit Servant.

Was it not yesterday we spoke together?

FIRST MURTHERER: It was, so please your Highness.

MACBETH: Well then,
Now have you consider'd of my speeches?
Know, that it was he in the times past
Which held you so under fortune,

Which you thought had been our innocent self?
This I made good to you in our last conference,
Pass'd in probation with you:
How you were borne in hand, how cross'd:
The instruments: who wrought with them,
And all things else that might
To half a soul and to a notion crazed,
Say, "Thus did Banquo."

FIRST MURTHERER: You made it known to us.

MACBETH: I did so, and went further, which is now
Our point of second meeting.
Do you find your patience so predominant
In your nature, that you can let this go?
Are you so gospel'd, to pray for this good man
And for his issue, whose heavy hand
Hath bow'd you to the grave
And beggar'd yours forever?

FIRST MURTHERER: We are men, my Liege.

MACBETH: Ay, in the catalogue ye go for men,
As hounds and greyhounds, mongrels, spaniels, curs,
Shoughs, waterrugs, and demi-wolves are clept
All by the name of dogs. The valued file
Distinguishes the swift, the slow, the subtle,
The housekeeper, the hunter, every one
According to the gift which bounteous nature
Hath in him closed, whereby he does receive

Particular addition, from the bill
That writes them all alike; and so of men.
Now if you have a station in the file,
Not i' th' worst rank of manhood, say it,
And I will put that business in your bosoms
Whose execution takes your enemy off,
Grapples you to the heart and love of us,
Who wear our health but sickly in his life,
Which in his death were perfect.

SECOND MURTHERER: I am one, my Liege,
Whom the vile blows and buffets of the world
Hath so incensed that I am reckless what
I do, to spite the world.

FIRST MURTHERER: And I another,
So weary with disasters, tugg'd with Fortune,
That I would set my life on any chance,
To mend it or be rid on't.

MACBETH: Both of you know Banquo was your enemy.

BOTH MURTHERERS: True, my Lord.

MACBETH: So is he mine, and in such bloody distance
That every minute of his being thrusts
Against my near'st of life; and though I could
With barefaced power sweep him from my sight,
And bid my will avouch it, yet I must not,
For certain friends that are both his and mine,
Whose loves I may not drop, but wail his fall

Who I myself struck down. And thence it is,
That I to your assistance do make love,
Masking the business from the common eye
For sundry weighty reasons.

SECOND MURTHERER: We shall, my Lord,
Perform what you command us.

FIRST MURTHERER: Though our lives,

MACBETH: Your spirits shine through you.
Within this hour at most
I will advise you where to plant yourselves,
Acquaint you with the perfect spy o' th' time,
The moment on't; fort must be done tonight
And something fro't the palace (always thought
That I require a clearness); and with him,
To leave no rubs nor botches in the work,
Fleance his son, that keeps him company,
Whose absence is no less material to me
Than is his father's, must embrace the fate
Of that dark hour. Resolve yourselves apart;
I'll come to you anon.

BOTH MURTHERERS: We are resolved, my Lord.

MACBETH: I'll call upon you straight. Abide within.
It is concluded: Banquo, thy soul's flight,
If it find Heaven, must find it out tonight.

Exit.

III. 2

Enter Lady Macbeth and a Servant.

LADY MACBETH: Is Banquo gone from Court?

SERVANT: Ay, madam, but returns again tonight.

LADY MACBETH: Say to the King I would attend his leisure
For a few words.

SERVANT: Madam, I will.

Exit.

LADY MACBETH: Nought's had, all's spent,
Where our desire is got without content.
'Tis safer to be that which we destroy
Than by destruction dwell in doubtful joy.

Enter Macbeth.

How now, my Lord? Why do you keep alone,
Of sorriest fancies your companions making,
Using those thoughts which should indeed have died
With them they think on? Things without all remedy
Should be without regard. What's done is done.

MACBETH: We have scotch'd the snake, not kill'd it.
She'll close and be herself, whilst our poor malice
Remains in danger of her former tooth.
But let the frame of things disjoint, both the worlds suffer,
Ere we will eat our meal in fear and sleep
In the affliction of these terrible dreams
That shake us nightly. Better be with the dead,

Whom we, to gain our peace, have sent to peace,
Than on the torture of the mind to lie
In restless ecstasy.
Duncan is in his grave;
After life's fitful fever he sleeps well,
Treason has done his worst; nor steel, nor poison,
Malice domestic, foreign levy, nothing,
Can touch him further.

LADY MACBETH: Come on,
Gentle my Lord, sleek o'er your rugged looks;
Be bright and jovial among your guests tonight.

MACBETH: So shall I, love, and so, I pray, be you.
Let your remembrance apply to Banquo;
Present him eminence, both with eye and tongue:
Unsafe the while, that we must lave,
Our honours in these flattering streams,
And make our faces vizards to our hearts,
Disguising what they are.

LADY MACBETH: You must leave this.

MACBETH: O, full of scorpions is my mind, dear wife!
Thou know'st that Banquo and his Fleance lives.

LADY MACBETH: But in them, Nature's copy's not eterne.

MACBETH: There's comfort yet; they are assailable.
Then be thou jocund. Ere the bat hath flown
His cloister'd flight, ere to black Hecat's summons
The shard-borne beetle with his drowsy hums,

Hath rung night's yawning peal, there shall be done
A deed of dreadful note.

LADY MACBETH: What's to be done?

MACBETH: Be innocent of the knowledge, dearest chuck,
Till thou applaud the deed. Come, seeling night,
Scarf up the tender eye of pitiful day,
And with thy bloody and invisible hand
Cancel and tear to pieces that great bond,
Which keeps me pale! Light thickens, and the crow
Makes wing to the rooky wood;
Good things of day begin to droop and drowse,
Whiles night's black agents to their preys do rouse.
Thou marvel'st at my words, but hold thee still:
Things bad begun make strong themselves by ill.
So, prithee, go with me.

Exeunt.

III. 3

Enter three Murtherers.

FIRST MURTHERER: But who did bid thee join with us?

THIRD MURTHERER: Macbeth.

SECOND MURTHERER: He needs not our mistrust, since he delivers
Our offices and what we have to do
To the direction just.

FIRST MURTHERER: Then stand with us.

The west yet glimmers with some streaks of day;
Now spurs the lated traveller apace
To gain the timely inn, and near approaches
The subject of our watch.

THIRD MURTHERER: Hark! I hear horses.

BANQUO: Give us a light there, hoa!

SECOND MURTHERER: Then 'tis he;
The rest that are within the note of expectation
Already are i' the Court.

FIRST MURTHERER: His horses go about.

THIRD MURTHERER: Almost a mile, but he does usually,
So all men do, from hence to the Palace gate
Make it their walk.

Enter Banquo, and Fleance with a torch.

SECOND MURTHERER: A light, a light!

THIRD MURTHERER: 'Tis he.

FIRST MURTHERER: Stand to't.

BANQUO: It will be rain tonight.

FIRST MURTHERER: Let it come down.
(They set upon Banquo)

BANQUO: O, treachery! Fly, good Fleance, fly, fly, fly!
Thou mayst revenge. O slave!

THIRD MURTHERER: Who did strike out the light?

FIRST MURTHERER: Wast not the way?

THIRD MURTHERER: There's but one down; the son is fled.

SECOND MURTHERER: We have lost

Best half of our affair.

FIRST MURTHERER: Well, let's away and say how much is done.

Exeunt.

III. 4

Banquet prepared. Enter Macbeth, Lady Macbeth, Ross, Lennox, Lords, and Attendants.

MACBETH: You know your own degrees; sit down.
At first and last, the hearty welcome.

LORDS: Thanks to your Majesty.

MACBETH: Ourself will mingle with society
And play the humble host.
Our hostess keeps her state, but in best time
We will require her welcome.

LADY MACBETH: Pronounce it for me, sir, to all our friends,
For my heart speaks, they are welcome.

Enter first Murtherer

MACBETH: See, they encounter thee with their hearts' thanks.
Both sides are even; here I'll sit i' th' midst.
Be large in mirth; anon we'll drink a measure
The table round. There's blood upon thy face.

MURTHERER: 'Tis Banquo's then.

MACBETH: 'Tis better thee without, than he within.
Is he dispatch'd?

MURTHERER: My Lord, his throat is cut; that I did for him.
MACBETH: Thou art the best o' th' cut-throats!
Yet he's good that did the like for Fleance.
If thou didst it, thou art the nonpareil.
MURTHERER: Most Royal Sir,
Fleance is 'scaped.
MACBETH: Then comes my fit again.
I had else been perfect,
Whole as the marble, founded as the rock,
As broad and general as the casing air;
But now I am cabin'd, cribb'd, confin'd, bound in
To saucy doubts and fears. But Banquo's safe?
MURTHERER: Ay, my good Lord. Safe in a ditch he bides,
With twenty trenched gashes on his head,
The least a death to nature.
MACBETH: Thanks for that.
There the grown serpent lies; the worm that's fled
Hath nature that in time will venom breed,
No teeth for the present. Get thee gone. Tomorrow
We'll hear ourselves again.

Exit Murtherer.

LADY MACBETH: My Royal Lord,
You do not give the cheer. The feast is sold
That is not often vouch'd, while 'tis a-making,
'Tis given with welcome. To feed were best at home;
From thence the sauce to meat is ceremony;

Meeting were bare without it.

Enter the Ghost of Banquo, and sits in Macbeth's place

MACBETH: Sweet remembrancer!
Now good digestion wait on appetite,
And health on both!

LENNOX: May't please your Highness sit.

MACBETH: Here had we now our country's honor roof'd,
Were the graced person of our Banquo present,
Who may I rather challenge for unkindness
Than pity for mischance!

ROSS: His absence, Sir,
Lays blame upon his promise. Please't your Highness
To grace us with your royal company?

MACBETH: The table's full.

LENNOX: Here is a place reserved, Sir.

MACBETH: Where?

LENNOX: Here, my good Lord.
What is't that moves your Highness?

MACBETH: Which of you have done this?

LORDS: What, my good Lord?

MACBETH: Thou canst not say I did it; never shake
Thy gory locks at me.

ROSS: Gentlemen, rise; his Highness is not well.

LADY MACBETH: Sit, worthy friends; my Lord is often thus,
And hath been from his youth. Pray you, keep seat.

The fit is momentary; upon a thought
He will again be well. If much you note him,
You shall offend him and extend his passion.
Feed, and regard him not. Are you a man?

MACBETH: Ay, and a bold one, that dare look on that
Which might appal the Devil.

LADY MACBETH: O proper stuff!
This is the very painting of your fear;
This is the air-drawn dagger which you said
Led you to Duncan. O, these flaws and starts,
(Impostors to true fear) would well become
A woman's story at a winter's fire,
Authorized by her grandam. Shame itself!
Why do you make such faces? When all's done,
You look but on a stool.

MACBETH: Prithee, see there!
Behold! Look! Lo, how say you?
Why, what care I? If thou canst nod, speak too.
If charnel houses and our graves must send
Those that we bury back, our monuments
Shall be the maws of kites.

Exit Ghost.

LADY MACBETH: What, quite unmann'd in folly?

MACBETH: If I stand here, I saw him.

LADY MACBETH: Fie, for shame!

MACBETH: Blood hath been shed ere now, i' the olden time,

Ere humane statute purged the gentle weal;
Ay, and since too, murthers have been perform'd
Too terrible for the ear. The time has been,
That, when the brains were out, the man would die,
And there an end; but now they rise again,
With twenty mortal murthers on their crowns,
And push us from our stools. This is more strange
Than such a murther is.

LADY MACBETH: My worthy Lord,
Your noble friends do lack you.

MACBETH: I do forget.
Do not muse at me, my most worthy friends.
I have a strange infirmity, which is nothing
To those that know me. Come, love and health to all;
Then I'll sit down. Give me some wine, fill full.

Enter Ghost.

I drink to the general joy o' th' whole table,
And to our dear friend Banquo, whom we miss.
Would he were here! To all and him we thirst,
And all to all.

LORDS: Our duties and the pledge.

MACBETH: Avaunt, and quit my sight! Let the earth hide thee!
Thy bones are marrowless, thy blood is cold;
Thou hast no speculation in those eyes
Which thou dost glare with.

LADY MACBETH: Think of this, good Peers,

But as a thing of custom. 'Tis no other,
Only it spoils the pleasure of the time.

MACBETH: What man dare, I dare:
Approach thou like the rugged Russian bear,
The arm'd rhinoceros, or the Hyrcan tiger;
Take any shape but that, and my firm nerves
Shall never tremble. Or be alive again,
And dare me to the desert with thy sword.
If trembling I inhabit then, protest me
The baby of a girl. Hence, horrible shadow!
Unreal mockery, hence!

Exit Ghost.

Why so, being gone,
I am a man again. Pray you sit still.

LADY MACBETH: You have displaced the mirth,
Broke the good meeting, with most admired disorder.

MACBETH: Can such things be,
And overcome us like a summer's cloud,
Without our special wonder? You make me strange
Even to the disposition that I owe
When now I think you can behold such sights
And keep the natural ruby of your cheeks,
When mine is blanch'd with fear.

ROSS: What sights, my Lord?

LADY MACBETH: I pray you, speak not; he grows worse
and worse;

Question enrages him. At once, good night.
Stand not upon the order of your going,
But go at once.

LENNOX: Good night, and better health
Attend his Majesty!

LADY MACBETH: A kind good night to all!

Exit Lords

MACBETH: It will have blood; they say
Blood will have blood:
Stones have been known to move and trees to speak;
Augures and understood relations, have
By maggot pies and choughs and rooks brought forth
The secret'st man of blood. What is the night?

LADY MACBETH: Almost at odds with morning, which is which.

MACBETH: How say'st thou, that Macduff denies his person
At our great bidding?

LADY MACBETH: Did you send to him, Sir?

MACBETH: I hear it by the way, but I will send:
There's not a one of them but in his house
I keep a servant feed. I will tomorrow,
(And betimes I will) to the weird sisters.
More shall they speak; for now I am bent to know,
By the worst means, the worst. For mine own good,
All causes shall give way. I am in blood
Stepp'd in so far that, should I wade no more,

Returning were as tedious as go o'er:
Strange things I have in head that will to hand,
Which must be acted, ere they may be scann'd.

LADY MACBETH: You lack the season of all natures, sleep.

MACBETH: Come, we'll to sleep. My strange and self-abuse
Is the initiate fear that wants hard use.
We are yet but young in deed.

Exeunt.

III. 5

Enter the three Witches, meeting Hecat.

FIRST WITCH: Why, how now, Hecat? You look angerly?

HECAT: Have I not reason, beldams as you are,
Saucy and overbold? How did you dare
To trade and traffic with Macbeth,
In riddles and affairs of death,
And I, the mistress of your charms,
The close contriver of all harms,
Was never call'd to bear my part,
Or show the glory of our art?
And, which is worse, all you have done
Hath been but for a wayward son,
Spiteful and wrathful, who, as others do,
Loves for his own ends, not for you.
But make amends now. Get you gone,
And at the pit of Acheron

Meet me i' th' morning, thither he
Will come to know his destiny.
Your vessels and your spells provide,
Your charms and everything beside.
I am for th' air; this night I'll spend
Unto a dismal and a fatal end.
Great business must be wrought ere noon:
Upon the corner of the moon
There hangs a vaporous drop profound;
I'll catch it ere it come to ground.
And that distill'd by magic sleights
Shall raise such artificial sprites
As by the strength of their illusion,
Shall draw him on to his confusion.
He shall spurn fate, scorn death, and bear
His hopes 'bove wisdom, grace, and fear.
And you all know security
Is mortals' chiefest enemy.

Music and a song

Hark! I am call'd; my little spirit, see,
Sits in a foggy cloud and stays for me.

Song within 'Come away, come away,' etc.

FIRST WITCH: Come, let's make haste; she'll soon be Back again.

Exeunt.

III. 6

Enter Lennox and another Lord.

LENNOX: My former speeches
Have but hit your thoughts,
Which can interpret farther; only I say
Thing's have been strangely borne. The gracious Duncan
Was pitied of Macbeth; marry, he was dead.
And the right valiant Banquo walk'd too late,
Whom, you may say, if't please you, Fleance kill'd,
For Fleance fled. Men must not walk too late.
Who cannot want the thought, how monstrous
It was for Malcolm and for Donalbain
To kill their gracious father? Damned fact!
How it did grieve Macbeth! Did he not straight,
In pious rage, the two delinquents tear
That were the slaves of drink and thralls of sleep?
Was not that nobly done? Ay, and wisely too,
For 'twould have anger'd any heart alive
To hear the men deny't. So that, I say,
He has borne all things well; and I do think
That, had he Duncan's sons under his key,
(As, an't please Heaven, he shall not) they should find
What 'twere to kill a father; so should Fleance.
But, peace! For from broad words, and 'cause he fail'd

His presence at the tyrant's feast, I hear,
Macduff lives in disgrace. Sir, can you tell
Where he bestows himself?
LORD: The son of Duncan,
From whom this tyrant holds the due of birth,
Lives in the English Court and is received
Of the most pious Edward with such grace
That the malevolence of fortune nothing
Takes from his high respect. Thither Macduff
Is gone to pray the holy King, upon his aid
To wake Northumberland and warlike Siward;
That by the help of these, (with Him above
To ratify the work) we may again
Give to our tables meat, sleep to our nights,
Free from our feasts and banquets bloody knives,
Do faithful homage, and receive free honors,
All which we pine for now. And this report
Hath so exasperate the King that he
Prepares for some attempt of war.
LENNOX: Sent he to Macduff?
LORD: He did, and with an absolute "Sir, not I,"
The cloudy messenger turns me his back,
And hums, as who should say, "You'll rue the time
That clogs me with this answer."
LENNOX: And that well might
Advise him to a caution, to hold what distance
His wisdom can provide. Some holy Angel
Fly to the Court of England and unfold

His message ere he come, that a swift blessing
May soon return to this our suffering country,
Under a hand accursed!
LORD: I'll send my prayers with him.

Exeunt.

IV. 1

Thunder. Enter the three Witches.

FIRST WITCH: Thrice the brinded cat hath mew'd.
SECOND WITCH: Thrice and once the hedge-pig whin'd
THIRD WITCH: Harpier cries, 'Tis time, 'tis time.
FIRST WITCH: Round about th' cauldron go;
In the poison'd entrails throw.
Toad, that under cold stone
Days and nights has thirty-one
Swelter'd venom sleeping got,
Boil thou first i' th' charmed pot.
ALL: Double, double, toil and trouble;
Fire burn and cauldron bubble.
SECOND WITCH: Fillet of a fenny snake,
In the cauldron boil and bake;
Eye of newt and toe of frog,
Wool of bat and tongue of dog,
Adder's fork and blind-worm's sting,
Lizard's leg and howlet's wing,
For a charm of powerful trouble,
Like a hell-broth boil and bubble.

ALL: Double, double, toil and trouble;
Fire burn and cauldron bubble.
THIRD WITCH: Scale of dragon, tooth of wolf,
Witch's mummy, maw and gulf
Of the ravin'd salt-sea shark,
Root of hemlock digg'd i' th' dark,
Liver of blaspheming Jew,
Gall of goat and slips of yew
Sliver'd in the moon's eclipse,
Nose of Turk and Tartar's lips,
Finger of birth-strangled babe
Ditch-deliver'd by a drab,
Make the gruel thick and slab.
Add thereto a tiger's chaudron,
For the ingredients of our cauldron.
ALL: Double, double, toil and trouble;
Fire burn and cauldron bubble.
SECOND WITCH: Cool it with a baboon's blood,
Then the charm is firm and good.

Enter Hecat to the other three Witches.

HECAT: O, well done! I commend your pains,
And everyone shall share i' th' gains.
And now about the cauldron sing,
Like elves and fairies in a ring,
Enchanting all that you put in.

Music and a song, "Black spirits."

SECOND WITCH: By the pricking of my thumbs,
Something wicked this way comes.
Open, locks,
Whoever knocks!

Enter Macbeth.

MACBETH: How now, you secret, black, and midnight hags?
What is't you do?

ALL: A deed without a name.

MACBETH: I conjure you, by that which you profess
(Howeer you come to know it) answer me:
Though you untie the winds and let them fight
Against the churches, though the yesty waves
Confound and swallow navigation up,
Though bladed corn be lodged and trees blown down,
Though castles topple on their warders' heads,
Though palaces and pyramids do slope
Their heads to their foundations, though the treasure
Of nature's germaine tumble all together
Even till destruction sicken, answer me
To what I ask you.

FIRST WITCH: Speak.

SECOND WITCH: Demand.

THIRD WITCH: We'll answer.

FIRST WITCH: Say, if thou'dst rather hear it from our mouths,

Or from our masters'?
MACBETH: Call 'em, let me see 'em.
FIRST WITCH: Pour in sow's blood that hath eaten
Her nine farrow; grease that's sweaten
From the murtherer's gibbet' throw
Into the flame.
ALL: Come, high or low;
Thyself and office deftly show!

Thunder. First Apparition: an armed Head.

MACBETH: Tell me, thou unknown power,
FIRST WITCH: He knows thy thought:
Hear his speech, but say thou nought.
FIRST APPARITION: Macbeth! Macbeth! Macbeth!
Beware Macduff,
Beware the Thane of Fife. Dismiss me. Enough.

He Descends.

MACBETH: Whate'er thou art, for thy good caution, thanks;
Thou hast harp'd my fear aright. But one word more.
FIRST WITCH: He will not be commanded. Here's an other,
More potent than the first.

Thunder. Second Apparition: a bloody Child.

SECOND APPARITION: Macbeth! Macbeth! Macbeth!
MACBETH: Had I three ears, I'd hear thee.
SECOND APPARITION: Be bloody, bold, and resolute: laugh to scorn

The power of man, for none of woman born
Shall harm Macbeth.

Descends.

MACBETH: Then live, Macduff. What need I fear of thee?
But yet I'll make assurance double sure,
And take a bond of fate: thou shalt not live,
That I may tell pale-hearted fear it lies,
And sleep in spite of thunder.

Thunder. Third Apparition: a Child crowned, with a tree in his hand.

What is this, that rises like the issue of a King,
And wears upon his baby-brow the round
And top of sovereignty?

ALL: Listen, but speak not to't.

THIRD APPARITION: Be lion-mettled, proud, and take no care
Who chafes, who frets, or where conspirers are:
Macbeth shall never vanquish'd be until
Great Birnam Wood to high Dunsinane Hill
Shall come against him.

Descends.

MACBETH: That will never be:
Who can impress the forest, bid the tree
Unfix his earth-bound root? Sweet bodements, good!
Rebellion's head, rise never till the Wood
Of Birnam rise, and our high-placed Macbeth
Shall live the lease of nature, pay his breath

To time and mortal custom. Yet my heart
Throbs to know one thing: tell me, if your Art
Can tell so much, shall Banquo's issue ever
Reign in this kingdom?

ALL: Seek to know no more.

MACBETH: I will be satisfied! Deny me this,
And an eternal curse fall on you! Let me know.
Why sinks that cauldron, and what noise is this?

Oboes

FIRST WITCH: Show!

SECOND WITCH: Show!

THIRD WITCH: Show!

ALL: Show his eyes, and grieve his heart;
Come like shadows, so depart!

A show of eight Kings, the last with a glass in his hand; Banquo's Ghost following.

MACBETH: Thou art too like the spirit of Banquo: down!
Thy crown does sear mine eyeballs. And thy hair,
Thou other gold-bound brow, is like the first.
A third is like the former. Filthy hags!
Why do you show me this? A fourth! Start, eyes!
What, will the line stretch out to the crack of doom?
Another yet! A seventh! I'll see no more!
And yet the eighth appears, who bears a glass,
Which shows me many more; and some I see,
That twofold balls and treble sceptres carry.

Horrible sight! Now I see 'tis true;
For the blood-bolter'd Banquo smiles upon me,
And points at them for his. What, is this so?

FIRST WITCH: Ay, Sir, all this is so. But why
Stands Macbeth thus amazedly?
Come, sisters, cheer we up his sprites,
And show the best of our delights.
I'll charm the air to give a sound,
While you perform your antic round,
That this great King may kindly say,
Our duties did his welcome pay.

Music. The Witches dance and vanish.

MACBETH: Where are they? Gone? Let this pernicious hour
Stand aye accursed in the calendar!
Come in, without there!

Enter Lennox.

LENNOX: What's your Grace's will?

MACBETH: Saw you the weird sisters?

LENNOX: No, my Lord.

MACBETH: Came they not by you?

LENNOX: No indeed, my Lord.

MACBETH: Infected be the air whereon they ride,
And damn'd all those that trust them! I did hear
The galloping of horse. Who was't came by?

LENNOX: 'Tis two or three, my Lord, that bring you word
Macduff is fled to England.

MACBETH: Fled to England?

LENNOX: Ay, my good Lord.

MACBETH: Time, thou anticipat'st my dread exploits.
The flighty purpose never is o'ertook
Unless the deed go with it. From this moment
The very firstlings of my heart shall be
The firstlings of my hand. And even now,
To crown my thoughts with acts, be it thought and done:
The castle of Macduff I will surprise,
Seize upon Fife, give to the edge o' th' sword
His wife, his babes, and all unfortunate souls
That trace him in his line. No boasting like a fool;
This deed I'll do before this purpose cool.
But no more sights! Where are these gentlemen?
Come, bring me where they are.

Exeunt.

IV. 2

Enter Lady Macduff, her Son, and Ross.

LADY MACDUFF: What had he done, to make him fly the land?

ROSS: You must have patience, Madam.

LADY MACDUFF: He had none;
His flight was madness. When our actions do not,
Our fears do make us traitors.

ROSS: You know not
Whether it was his wisdom or his fear.
LADY MACDUFF: Wisdom? To leave his wife, to leave his babes,
His mansion, and his titles, in a place
From whence himself does fly? He loves us not;
He wants the natural touch; for the poor wren,
(The most diminutive of birds) will fight,
Her young ones in her nest, against the owl.
All is the fear and nothing is the love;
As little is the wisdom, where the flight
So runs against all reason.
ROSS: My dearest coz,
I pray you, school yourself. But for your husband,
He is noble, wise, judicious, and best knows
The fits o' th' season. I dare not speak much further;
But cruel are the times when we are traitors
And do not know ourselves; when we hold rumour
From what we fear, yet know not what we fear,
But float upon a wild and violent sea
Each way and move. I take my leave of you;
Shall not be long but I'll be here again.
Things at the worst will cease or else climb upward
To what they were before. My pretty cousin,
Blessing upon you!
LADY MACDUFF: Father'd he is, and yet he's fatherless.

ROSS: I am so much a fool, should I stay longer,
It would be my disgrace and your discomfort.
I take my leave at once.

Exit Ross

LADY MACDUFF: Sirrah, your father's dead.
And what will you do now? How will you live?
SON: As birds do, Mother.
LADY MACDUFF: What, with worms and flies?
SON: With what I get, I mean; and so do they.
LADY MACDUFF: Poor bird!
Thou'ldst never fear the net nor lime,
The pitfall nor the gin.
SON: Why should I, Mother?
Poor birds they are not set for.
My father is not dead, for all your saying.
LADY MACDUFF: Yes, he is dead.
How wilt thou do for father?
SON: Nay, how will you do for a husband?
LADY MACDUFF: Why, I can buy me twenty at any market.
SON: Then you'll buy 'em to sell again.
LADY MACDUFF: Thou speak'st with all thy wit, and yet, i' faith,
With wit enough for thee.
SON: Was my father a traitor, Mother?
LADY MACDUFF: Ay, that he was.
SON: What is a traitor?

LADY MACDUFF: Why one that swears and lies.

SON: And be all traitors that do so?

LADY MACDUFF: Everyone that does so is a traitor and must be hang'd.

SON: And must they all be hang'd that swear and lie?

LADY MACDUFF: Everyone.

SON: Who must hang them?

LADY MACDUFF: Why, the honest men.

SON: Then the liars and swearers are fools, for there are liars and swearers enow to beat the honest men and hang up them.

LADY MACDUFF: Now, God help thee, poor monkey!
But how wilt thou do for a father?

SON: If he were dead, you'ld weep for him; if you would not, it were a good sign that I should quickly have a new father.

LADY MACDUFF: Poor prattler, how thou talk'st!

Enter a Messenger.

MESSENGER: Bless you, fair Dame! I am not to you known,
Though in your state of honour I am perfect.
I doubt some danger does approach you nearly.
If you will take a homely man's advice,
Be not found here; hence, with your little ones.
To fright you thus, methinks I am too savage;
To do worse to you were fell cruelty,
Which is too nigh your person. Heaven preserve you!
I dare abide no longer.

Exit Messenger

LADY MACDUFF: Whither should I fly?
I have done no harm. But I remember now
I am in this earthly world, where to do harm
Is often laudable, to do good sometime
Accounted dangerous folly. Why then, alas,
Do I put up that womanly defense,
To say I have done no harm? What are these faces?

Enter Murtherers.

FIRST MURTHERER: Where is your husband?

LADY MACDUFF: I hope, in no place so unsanctified
Where such as thou mayst find him.

FIRST MURTHERER: He's a traitor.

SON: Thou liest, thou shag-ear'd villain!

FIRST MURTHERER: What, you egg!
Young fry of treachery!
(Stabs him)

SON: He has kill'd me, Mother.
Run away, I pray you! (Dies.)

Exit crying "Murther!"

IV. 3

Enter Malcolm and Macduff.

MALCOLM: Let us seek out some desolate shade and there
Weep our sad bosoms empty.

MACDUFF: Let us rather

Hold fast the mortal sword, and like good men
Bestride our downfall'n birthdom. Each new morn
New widows howl, new orphans cry, new sorrows
Strike heaven on the face, that it resounds
As if it felt with Scotland and yell'd out
Like syllable of dolor.

MALCOLM: What I believe, I'll wail;
What know, believe; and what I can redress,
As I shall find the time to friend, I will.
What you have spoke, it may be so perchance.
This tyrant, whose sole name blisters our tongues,
Was once thought honest. You have loved him well;
He hath not touch'd you yet. I am young, but something
You may discesn of him through me, and wisdom
To offer up a weak, poor, innocent lamb
To appease an angry god.

MACDUFF: I am not treacherous.

MALCOLM: But Macbeth is.
A good and virtuous nature may recoil
In an imperial charge. But I shall crave your pardon;
That which you are, my thoughts cannot transpose.
Angels are bright still, though the brightest fell.
Though all things foul, would wear the brows of grace,
Yet grace must still look so.

MACDUFF: I have lost my hopes.

MALCOLM: Perchance even there where I did find my doubts.

Why in that rawness left you wife and child?
Those precious motives, those strong knots of love,
Without leave-taking? I pray you,
Let not my jealousies be your dishonours,
But mine own safeties. You may be rightly just,
Whatever I shall think.

MACDUFF: Bleed, bleed, poor country!
Great tyranny, lay thou thy basis sure,
For goodness dare not check thee. Wear thou thy wrongs;
The title is affeer'd. Fare thee well, Lord.
I would not be the villain that thou think'st
For the whole space that's in the tyrant's grasp
And the rich East to boot.

MALCOLM: Be not offended;
I speak not as in absolute fear of you:
I think our country sinks beneath the yoke;
It weeps, it bleeds, and each new day a gash
Is added to her wounds. I think withal,
There would be hands uplifted in my right;
And here from gracious England have I offer
Of goodly thousands. But for all this,
When I shall tread upon the tyrant's head,
Or wear it on my sword, yet my poor country
Shall have more vices than it had before,
More suffer and more sundry ways than ever,

By him that shall succeed.
MACDUFF: What should he be?
MALCOLM: It is myself I mean, in whom I know
All the particulars of vice so grafted,
That, when they shall be open'd, black Macbeth
Will seem as pure as snow, and the poor state
Esteem him as a lamb, being compar'd
With my confineless harms.
MACDUFF: Not in the legions
Of horrid Hell, can come a devil more damn'd
In evils to top Macbeth.
MALCOLM: I grant him bloody,
Luxurious, avaricious, false, deceitful,
Sudden, malicious, smacking of every sin
That has a name. But there's no bottom, none,
In my voluptuousness. Your wives, your daughters,
Your matrons, and your maids could not fill up
The cistern of my lust, and my desire
All continent impediments would o'erbear
That did oppose my will. Better Macbeth
Than such an one to reign.
MACDUFF: Boundless intemperance
In Nature is a tyranny; it hath been
The untimely emptying of the happy throne,
And fall of many kings. But fear not yet
To take upon you what is yours. You may

Convey your pleasures in a spacious plenty
And yet seem cold, the time you may so hoodwink.
We have willing dames enough; there cannot be
That vulture in you to devour so many
As will to greatness dedicate themselves,
Finding it so inclined.

MALCOLM: With this there grows
In my most ill-composed affection, such
A stanchless avarice that, were I King,
I should cut off the Nobles for their lands,
Desire his jewels and this other's house,
And my more-having would be as a sauce
To make me hunger more, that I should forge
Quarrels unjust against the good and loyal,
Destroying them for wealth.

MACDUFF: This avarice
Sticks deeper, grows with more pernicious root
Than summer-seeming lust, and it hath been
The sword of our slain Kings. Yet do not fear;
Scotland hath foisons to fill up your will
Of your mere own. All these are portable,
With other graces weigh'd.

MALCOLM: But I have none. The king-becoming graces,
As justice, verity, temperance, stableness,
Bounty, perseverance, mercy, lowliness,
Devotion, patience, courage, fortitude,

I have no relish of them, but abound
In the division of each several crime,
Acting it many ways. Nay, had I power, I should
Pour the sweet milk of concord into Hell,
Uproar the universal peace, confound
All unity on earth.

MACDUFF: O Scotland, Scotland!

MALCOLM: If such a one be fit to govern, speak.
I am as I have spoken.

MACDUFF: Fit to govern?
No, not to live. O nation miserable!
With an untitled tyrant bloody-scepter'd,
When shalt thou see thy wholesome days again,
Since that the truest issue of thy Throne
By his own interdiction stands accursed
And does blaspheme his breed? Thy Royal Father
Was a most sainted King; the Queen that bore thee,
Oftener upon her knees than on her feet,
Died every day she lived. Fare thee well!
These evils thou repeat'st upon thyself
Have banish'd me from Scotland. O my breast,
Thy hope ends here!

MALCOLM: Macduff, this noble passion,
Child of integrity, hath from my soul
Wip'd the black scruples, reconcil'd my thoughts
To thy good truth and honor. Devilish Macbeth

By many of these trains, hath sought to win me
Into his power, and modest wisdom plucks me
From over-credulous haste. But God above
Deal between thee and me! For even now
I put myself to thy direction and
Unspeak mine own detraction; here abjure
The taints and blames I laid upon myself,
For strangers to my nature. I am yet
Unknown to woman, never was forsworn,
Scarcely have coveted what was mine own,
At no time broke my faith, would not betray
The Devil to his fellow, and delight
No less in truth than life. My first false speaking
Was this upon myself. What I am truly
Is thine and my poor country's to command.
Whither indeed, before thy here approach,
Old Siward, with ten thousand warlike men
Already at a point, was setting forth.
Now we'll together, and the chance of goodness
Be like our warranted quarrel! Why are you silent?

MACDUFF: Such welcome and unwelcome things at once
'Tis hard to reconcile.

Enter a Doctor.

MALCOLM: Well, more anon. Comes the King forth, I pray you?

DOCTOR: Ay, sir, there are a crew of wretched souls

That stay his cure. Their malady convinces
The great assay of art, but at his touch,
Such sanctity hath Heaven given his hand,
They presently amend.

MALCOLM: I thank you, Doctor.

Exit

MACDUFF: What's the disease he means?

MALCOLM: 'Tis call'd the Evil:
A most miraculous work in this good King,
Which often, since my here remain in England,
I have seen him do. How he solicits Heaven,
Himself best knows; but strangely-visited people,
All swol'n and ulcerous, pitiful to the eye,
The mere despair of surgery, he cures,
Hanging a golden stamp about their necks
Put on with holy prayers; and 'tis spoken,
To the succeeding royalty he leaves
The healing benediction. With this strange virtue
He hath a heavenly gift of prophecy,
And sundry blessings hang about his Throne
That speak him full of grace.

Enter Ross.

MACDUFF: See, who comes here?

MALCOLM: My countryman, but yet I know him not.

MACDUFF: My ever gentle cousin, welcome hither.

MALCOLM: I know him now. Good God, betimes remove

The means that makes us strangers!
ROSS: Sir, amen.
MACDUFF: Stands Scotland where it did?
ROSS: Alas, poor country,
Almost afraid to know itself! It cannot
Be call'd our mother, but our grave. Where nothing,
But who knows nothing, is once seen to smile;
Where sighs and groans and shrieks that rent the air,
Are made, not mark'd; where violent sorrow seems
A modern ecstasy. The dead man's knell
Is there scarce ask'd for who, and good men's lives
Expire before the flowers in their caps,
Dying or ere they sicken.
MACDUFF: O, relation
Too nice, and yet too true!
MALCOLM: What's the newest grief?
ROSS: That of an hour's age doth hiss the speaker;
Each minute teems a new one.
MACDUFF: How does my wife?
ROSS: Why, well.
MACDUFF: And all my children?
ROSS: Well too.
MACDUFF: The tyrant has not batter'd at their peace?
ROSS: No, they were well at peace when I did leave 'em.
MACDUFF: Be not a niggard of your speech. How goes't?
ROSS: When I came hither to transport the tidings,

Which I have heavily borne, there ran a rumor
Of many worthy fellows that were out,
Which was to my belief witness'd the rather,
For that I saw the tyrant's power a-foot.
Now is the time of help; your eye in Scotland
Would create soldiers, make our women fight,
To doff their dire distresses.

MALCOLM: Be't their comfort
We are coming thither. Gracious England hath
Lent us good Siward and ten thousand men;
An older and a better soldier none
That Christendom gives out.

ROSS: Would I could answer
This comfort with the like! But I have words
That would be howl'd out in the desert air,
Where hearing should not latch them.

MACDUFF: What concern they?
The general cause? Or is it a fee-grief
Due to some single breast?

ROSS: No mind that's honest
But in it shares some woe, though the main part
Pertains to you alone.

MACDUFF: If it be mine,
Keep it not from me, quickly let me have it.

ROSS: Let not your ears despise my tongue forever,
Which shall possess them with the heaviest sound

That ever yet they heard.
MACDUFF: Humh! I guess at it.
ROSS: Your castle is surprised; your wife and babes
Savagely slaughter'd. To relate the manner
Were on the quarry of these murther'd deer,
To add the death of you.
MALCOLM: Merciful Heaven!
What, man! Ne'er pull your hat upon your brows;
Give sorrow words. The grief that does not speak
Whispers the o'erfraught heart, and bids it break.
MACDUFF: My children too?
ROSS: Wife, children, servants, all
That could be found.
MACDUFF: And I must be from thence!
My wife kill'd too?
ROSS: I have said.
MALCOLM: Be comforted.
Let's make us medicines of our great revenge,
To cure this deadly grief.
MACDUFF: He has no children. All my pretty ones?
Did you say all? O hell-kite! All?
What, all my pretty chickens and their dam
At one fell swoop?
MALCOLM: Dispute it like a man.
MACDUFF: I shall do so,
But I must also feel it as a man.

I cannot but remember such things were
That were most precious to me. Did Heaven look on,
And would not take their part? Sinful Macduff,
They were all struck for thee! Naught that I am,
Not for their own demerits, but for mine,
Fell slaughter on their souls. Heaven rest them now!

MALCOLM: Be this the whetstone of your sword. Let
grief convert to anger; blunt not the heart, enrage it.

MACDUFF: O, I could play the woman with mine eyes
And braggart with my tongue! But, gentle Heavens,
Cut short all intermission; front to front
Bring thou this fiend of Scotland and myself;
Within my sword's length set him; if he 'scape,
Heaven forgive him too!

MALCOLM: This tune goes manly.
Come, go we to the King; our Power is ready,
Our lack is nothing but our leave. Macbeth
Is ripe for shaking, and the Powers above
Put on their instruments. Receive what cheer you
may,
The night is long that never finds the day.

Exeunt.

V. 1

Enter a Doctor of Physic and a waiting Gentlewoman.

DOCTOR: I have two nights watched with you, but can perceive no truth in your report. When was it she last walked?

GENTLEWOMAN: Since his Majesty went into the field, I have seen her rise from her bed, throw her nightgown upon her, unlock her closet, take forth paper, fold it, write upon't, read it, afterwards seal it, and again return to bed; yet all this while in a most fast sleep.

DOCTOR: A great perturbation in nature, to receive at once the benefit of sleep and do the effects of watching! In this slumbery agitation, besides her walking and other actual performances, what, at any time, have you heard her say?

GENTLEWOMAN: That, sir, which I will not report after her.

DOCTOR: You may to me, and 'tis most meet you should.

GENTLEWOMAN: Neither to you nor anyone, having no witness to confirm my speech.

Enter Lady Macbeth with a taper.

Lo you, here she comes! This is her very guise, and, upon my life, fast asleep. Observe her; stand close.

DOCTOR: How came she by that light?

GENTLEWOMAN: Why, it stood by her. She has light by her continually; 'tis her command.

DOCTOR: You see, her eyes are open.

GENTLEWOMAN: Ay, but their sense are shut.

DOCTOR: What is it she does now?

Look how she rubs her hands.

GENTLEWOMAN: It is an accustomed action with her, to seem thus washing her hands. I have known her continue in this a quarter of an hour.

LADY MACBETH: Yet here's a spot.

DOCTOR: Hark, she speaks! I will set down what comes from her, to satisfy my remembrance the more strongly.

LADY MACBETH: Out, damned spot! Out, I say! One: two: why then 'tis time to do't. Hell is murky. Fie, my lord, fie! A soldier, and afear'd? What need we fear who knows it, when none can call our power to account? Yet who would have thought the old man to have had so much blood in him?

DOCTOR: Do you mark that?

LADY MACBETH: The Thane of Fife had a wife; where is she now? What, will these hands ne'er be clean? No more o' that, my Lord, no more o' that. You mar all with this starting.

DOCTOR: Go to, go to; you have known what you should not.

GENTLEWOMAN: She has spoke what she should not, I am sure of that.
Heaven knows what she has known.

LADY MACBETH: Here's the smell of the blood still. All the perfumes of Arabia will not sweeten this little hand. Oh, oh, oh!

DOCTOR: What a sigh is there! The heart is sorely charged.

GENTLEWOMAN: I would not have such a heart in my bosom, for the dignity of the whole body.

DOCTOR: Well, well, well.

GENTLEWOMAN: Pray God it be, sir.

DOCTOR: This disease is beyond my practice. Yet I have known those which have walked in their sleep who have died holily in their beds.

LADY MACBETH: Wash your hands, put on your night-gown, look not so pale. I tell you yet again, Banquo's buried; he cannot come out on's grave.

DOCTOR: Even so?

LADY MACBETH: To bed, to bed; there's knocking at the gate. Come, come, come, come, give me your hand. What's done cannot be undone. To bed, to bed, to bed.

Exit Lady Macbeth

DOCTOR: Will she go now to bed?

GENTLEWOMAN: Directly.

DOCTOR: Foul whisperings are abroad. Unnatural deeds
Do breed unnatural troubles; infected minds
To their deaf pillows will discharge their secrets.
More needs she the divine than the physician.
God, God, forgive us all! Look after her;
Remove from her the means of all annoyance,
And still keep eyes upon her. So good night.
My mind she has mated and amazed my sight.
I think, but dare not speak.

GENTLEWOMAN: Good night, good doctor.

Exeunt.

V. 2

Enter Menteith, Caithness, Angus, Lennox, and Soldiers.

MENTEITH: The English power is near, led on by Malcolm,
His uncle Siward, and the good Macduff.
Revenges burn in them, for their dear causes
Would to the bleeding and the grim alarm
Excite the mortified man.
ANGUS: Near Birnam Wood
Shall we well meet them; that way are they coming.
CAITHNESS: Who knows if Donalbain be with his brother?
LENNOX: For certain, sir, he is not; I have a file
Of all the gentry. There is Seward's son
And many unrough youths that even now
Protest their first of manhood.
MENTEITH: What does the tyrant?
CAITHNESS: Great Dunsinane he strongly fortifies.
Some say he's mad; others, that lesser hate him,
Do call it valiant fury; but, for certain,
He cannot buckle his distemper'd cause
Within the belt of rule.
ANGUS: Now does he feel
His secret murthers sticking on his hands,
Now minutely revolts upbraid his faith-breach;
Those he commands, move only in command,
Nothing in love. Now does he feel his title

Hang loose about him, like a giant's robe
Upon a dwarfish thief.

MENTEITH: Who then shall blame
His pester'd senses to recoil and start,
When all that is within him does condemn
Itself for being there?

CAITHNESS: Well, march we on,
To give obedience where 'tis truly owed.
Meet we the medicine of the sickly weal,
And with him pour we, in our country's purge,
Each drop of us.

LENNOX: Or so much as it needs
To dew the sovereign flower and drown the weeds.
Make we our march towards Birnam.

Exeunt marching.

V. 3

Enter Macbeth, Doctor, and Attendants.

MACBETH: Bring me no more reports; let them fly all!
Till Birnam Wood remove to Dunsinane
I cannot taint with fear. What's the boy Malcolm?
Was he not born of woman? The spirits that know
All mortal consequences have pronounced me thus:
"Fear not, Macbeth; no man that's born of woman
Shall e'er have power upon thee." Then fly, false
Thanes,
And mingle with the English epicures!

The mind I sway by and the heart I bear
Shall never sag with doubt nor shake with fear.

Enter a Servant.

The devil damn thee black, thou cream-faced loon!
Where got'st thou that goose look?

SERVANT: There is ten thousand.

MACBETH: Geese, villain?

SERVANT: Soldiers, sir.

MACBETH: Go prick thy face and over-red thy fear,
Thou lily-liver'd boy. What soldiers, patch?
Death of thy soul! Those linen cheeks of thine
Are counsellors to fear. What soldiers, whey-face?

SERVANT: The English force, so please you.

MACBETH: Take thy face hence.

Exit Servant.

Seyton, I am sick at heart,
When I behold: Seyton, I say, this push
Will cheer me ever or disseat me now.
I have lived long enough. My way of life
Is fall'n into the sear, the yellow leaf,
And that which should accompany old age,
As honour, love, obedience, troops of friends,
I must not look to have; but in their stead,
Curses, not loud but deep, mouth-honor, breath,
Which the poor heart would fain deny and dare not.
Seyton!

Enter Seyton.

SEYTON: What's your gracious pleasure?

MACBETH: What news more?

SEYTON: All is confirm'd, my Lord, which was reported.

MACBETH: I'll fight, till from my bones, my flesh be hack'd.
Give me my armour.

SEYTON: 'Tis not needed yet.

MACBETH: I'll put it on.
Send out more horses, skirr the country round,
Hang those that talk of fear. Give me mine armour.
How does your patient, doctor?

DOCTOR: Not so sick, my Lord,
As she is troubled with thick-coming fancies,
That keep her from her rest.

MACBETH: Cure her of that.
Canst thou not minister to a mind diseased,
Pluck from the memory a rooted sorrow,
Raze out the written troubles of the brain,
And with some sweet oblivious antidote
Cleanse the stuff'd bosom of that perilous stuff
Which weighs upon the heart?

DOCTOR: Therein the patient
Must minister to himself.

MACBETH: Throw physic to the dogs, I'll none of it.
Come, put mine armour on; give me my staff.
Seyton, send out. Doctor, the Thanes fly from me.

Come, sir, dispatch. If thou couldst, doctor, cast
The water of my land, find her disease
And purge it to a sound and pristine health,
I would applaud thee to the very echo,
That should applaud again. Pull't off, I say.
What rhubarb, senna or what purgative drug
Would scour these English hence? Hearst thou of them?

DOCTOR: Ay, my good Lord, your royal preparation
Makes us hear something.

MACBETH: Bring it after me.
I will not be afraid of death and bane,
Till Birnam Forest come to Dunsinane.

DOCTOR: Were I from Dunsinane away and clear,
Profit again should hardly draw me here.

Exeunt.

V. 4

Enter Malcolm, Siward and his Son, Macduff, Menteith, Caithness, Angus, Lennox, Ross, and Soldiers, marching.

MALCOLM: Cousins, I hope the days are near at hand
That chambers will be safe.

MENTEITH: We doubt it nothing.

SIWARD: What wood is this before us?

MENTEITH: The Wood of Birnam.

MALCOLM: Let every soldier hew him down a bough,

And bear't before him; thereby shall we shadow
The numbers of our host, and make discovery
Err in report of us.
SOLDIERS: It shall be done.
SIWARD: We learn no other but the confident tyrant
Keeps still in Dunsinane and will endure
Our setting down before't.
MALCOLM: 'Tis his main hope;
For where there is advantage to be given,
Both more and less have given him the revolt,
And none serve with him but constrained things
Whose hearts are absent too.
MACDUFF: Let our just censures
Attend the true event, and put we on
Industrious soldiership.
SIWARD: The time approaches
That will with due decision make us know
What we shall say we have and what we owe.
Thoughts speculative their unsure hopes relate,
But certain issue strokes must arbitrate.
Towards which advance the war.

Exeunt Marching.

V. 5

Enter Macbeth, Seyton, and Soldiers, with drum and colours.

MACBETH: Hang out our banners on the outward walls;
The cry is still, "They come!" Our castle's strength
Will laugh a siege to scorn. Here let them lie

Till famine and the ague eat them up.
Were they not forced with those that should be ours,
We might have met them dareful, beard to beard,
And beat them backward home.

A cry of women within.

What is that noise?

SEYTON: It is the cry of women, my good Lord.

MACBETH: I have almost forgot the taste of fears:
The time has been, my senses would have cool'd
To hear a night-shriek, and my fell of hair
Would at a dismal treatise rouse and stir
As life were in't. I have supp'd full with horrors;
Direness, familiar to my slaughterous thoughts,
Cannot once start me.
Wherefore was that cry?

SEYTON: The Queen, my Lord, is dead.

MACBETH: She should have died hereafter;
There would have been a time for such a word.
Tomorrow, and tomorrow, and tomorrow
Creeps in this petty pace from day to day
To the last syllable of recorded time;
And all our yesterdays have lighted fools
The way to dusty death. Out, out, brief candle!
Life's but a walking shadow, a poor player
That struts and frets his hour upon the stage
And then is heard no more. It is a tale

Told by an idiot, full of sound and fury,
Signifying nothing.

Enter a Messenger.

Thou comest to use thy tongue; thy story quickly.

MESSENGER: Gracious my Lord,
I should report that which I say I saw,
But know not how to do it.

MACBETH: Well, say, sir.

MESSENGER: As I did stand my watch upon the hill,
I look'd toward Birnam, and anon, methought,
The Wood began to move.

MACBETH: Liar and slave!

MESSENGER: Let me endure your wrath, if't be not so.
Within this three mile may you see it coming;
I say, a moving grove.

MACBETH: If thou speak'st false,
Upon the next tree shalt thou hang alive,
Till famine cling thee; if thy speech be sooth,
I care not if thou dost for me as much.
I pull in resolution and begin
To doubt the equivocation of the fiend
That lies like truth. "Fear not, till Birnam Wood
Do come to Dunsinane," and now a wood
Comes toward Dunsinane. Arm, arm, and out!
If this which he avouches does appear,
There is nor flying hence nor tarrying here.

I 'gin to be aweary of the sun
And wish the estate o' th' world were now undone.
Ring the alarum bell! Blow, wind! Come, wrack!
At least we'll die with harness on our back.

Exeunt.

V. 6

Enter Malcolm, Siward, Macduff, and their Army, with boughs. Drum and colours.

MALCOLM: Now near enough;
Your leavy screens throw down,
And show like those you are. You, worthy uncle,
Shall with my cousin, your right noble son,
Lead our first battle. Worthy Macduff and we
Shall take upon's what else remains to do,
According to our order.

SIWARD: Fare you well.
Do we but find the tyrant's power tonight,
Let us be beaten if we cannot fight.

MACDUFF: Make all our trumpets speak, give them all breath,
Those clamorous harbingers of blood and death.

Exeunt.

Alarums continued

V. 7

Enter Macbeth.

MACBETH: They have tied me to a stake; I cannot fly,
But bear-like I must fight the course. What's he
That was not born of woman? Such a one
Am I to fear, or none.

Enter young Siward.

YOUNG SIWARD: What is thy name?

MACBETH: Thou'lt be afraid to hear it.

YOUNG SIWARD: No, though thou call'st thyself a hotter name
Than any is in hell.

MACBETH: My name's Macbeth.

YOUNG SIWARD: The devil himself could not pronounce a title
More hateful to mine ear.

MACBETH: No, nor more fearful.

YOUNG SIWARD: O Thou liest, abhorred tyrant; with my sword
I'll prove the lie thou speak'st.

They fight, and young Siward is slain.

MACBETH: Thou wast born of woman.
But swords I smile at, weapons laugh to scorn,
Brandish'd by man that's of a woman born.

Exit.

Alarums. Enter Macduff.

MACDUFF: That way the noise is. Tyrant, show thy face!
If thou best slain and with no stroke of mine,

My wife and children's ghosts will haunt me still.
I cannot strike at wretched kerns, whose arms
Are hir'd to bear their staves. Either thou, Macbeth,
Or else my sword, with an unbatter'd edge,
I sheathe again undeeded. There thou shouldst be;
By this great clatter, one of greatest note
Seems bruited. Let me find him, Fortune!
And more I beg not.

Exit. Alarums.

Enter Malcolm and Siward.

SIWARD: This way, my Lord; the castle's gently render'd.
The tyrant's people on both sides do fight,
The noble Thanes do bravely in the war,
The day almost itself professes yours,
And little is to do.

MALCOLM: We have met with foes
That strike beside us.

SIWARD: Enter, Sir, the Castle.

Exeunt. Alarum.

Enter Macbeth.

MACBETH: Why should I play the Roman fool and die
On mine own sword? Whiles I see lives, the gashes
Do better upon them.

Enter Macduff.

MACDUFF: Turn, hell hound, turn!

MACBETH: Of all men else I have avoided thee.

But get thee back, my soul is too much charged
With blood of thine already.

MACDUFF: I have no words.
My voice is in my sword, thou bloodier villain
Than terms can give thee out! (They fight).

MACBETH: Thou losest labour.
As easy mayst thou the intrenchant air
With thy keen sword impress as make me bleed.
Let fall thy blade on vulnerable crests;
I bear a charmed life, which must not yield
To one of woman born.

MACDUFF: Despair thy charm,
And let the angel whom thou still hast serv'd
Tell thee, Macduff was from his mother's womb
Untimely ripp'd.

MACBETH: Accursed be that tongue that tells me so,
For it hath cow'd my better part of man!
And be these juggling fiends no more believed
That patter with us in a double sense,
That keep the word of promise to our ear
And break it to our hope. I'll not fight with thee.

MACDUFF: Then yield thee, coward,
And live to be the show and gaze o' th' time.
We'll have thee, as our rarer monsters are,
Painted upon a pole, and underwrit,
"Here may you see the tyrant."

MACBETH: I will not yield,
To kiss the ground before young Malcolm's feet,
And to be baited with the rabble's curse.
Though Birnam Wood be come to Dunsinane,
And thou oppos'd, being of no woman born,
Yet I will try the last. Before my body
I throw my warlike shield! Lay on, Macduff,
And damn'd be him that first cries, Hold, enough!

Exeunt fighting. Alarums.

Retreat and flourish. Enter, with drum and colours, Malcolm, Siward, Ross, Thanes, and Soldiers.

MALCOLM: I would the friends we miss were safe arrived.
SIWARD: Some must go off, and yet, by these I see,
So great a day as this is cheaply bought.
MALCOLM: Macduff is missing, and your noble son.
ROSS: Your son, my Lord, has paid a soldier's debt.
He only lived but till he was a man,
The which no sooner had his prowess confirm'd
In the unshrinking station where he fought,
But like a man he died.
SIWARD: Then he is dead?
ROSS: Ay, and brought off the field. Your cause of sorrow
Must not be measured by his worth, for then
It hath no end.
SIWARD: Had he his hurts before?
ROSS: Ay, on the front.

SIWARD: Why then, God's soldier be he!
Had I as many sons as I have hairs,
I would not wish them to a fairer death.
And so his knell is knoll'd.
MALCOLM: He's worth more sorrow,
And that I'll spend for him.
SIWARD: He's worth no more:
They say he parted well and paid his score,
And so God be with him! Here comes newer comfort.

Enter Macduff, with Macbeth's head.

MACDUFF: Hail, King, for so thou art.
Behold where stands
The usurper's cursed head. The time is free.
I see thee compass'd with thy Kingdom's pearl
That speak my salutation in their minds,
Whose voices I desire aloud with mine.
Hail, King of Scotland!
ALL: Hail, King of Scotland!

Flourish.

MALCOLM: We shall not spend a large expense of time
Before we reckon with your several loves
And make us even with you. My Thanes and kinsmen,
Henceforth be Earls, the first that ever Scotland
In such an honour named. What's more to do,
Which would be planted newly with the time,
As calling home our exiled friends abroad,

That fled the snares of watchful tyranny,
Producing forth the cruel ministers
Of this dead butcher and his fiend-like queen,
Who, as 'tis thought, by self and violent hands
Took off her life; this, and what needful else
That calls upon us, by the grace of Grace
We will perform in measure, time, and place.
So thanks to all at once and to each one,
Whom we invite to see us crown'd at Scone.

Flourish. Exeunt. omnes.

FINIS

GLOSSARY

addition: a title of honour added to the name, so *'honour'*

address'd: made ready

admir'd: wondered at

affeer'd: confirmed

all-thing: in every way

anon: 'I am coming'

annoyance: harm

antic: fantastic

approve: demonstrate

assay: effort

avouch: proclaim

badg'd: lit. wearing a badge of blood

bane: destruction

bare-fac'd: without concealment

battle: division (of an army)

beguile: deceive

beldams: ugly old woman

benison: blessing

blood-bolter'd: matted with blood

bodements: prophecies

borne: managed

botches: flaws

break: reveal

breech'd: covered as with breches

brinded: branded, striped

bruited: noise abroad

cabin'd: confined in a small room

card: the card marking the points of the compass

casing: enclosing

cast: throw up

charg'd: burdened

chaudron: entrails

choppy: chapped

chough: jackdaw

clear: innocent

clearness: freedom from suspicion

clept: called

cling: wither

closet: chest, used for private papers

coign of vantage: convenient corner

composition: agreement, terms of peace

compt: account, which must be produced at the audit

consent: party

continent: containing, restrainning

convince: overpower

corporal: bodily

cours'd: pursued

coz: cousin, kinsman

cracks: cannon-balls

crests: heads

cribb'd: confined in a crib

cross'd: thwarted

dear: heartfelt

demi-wolves: half-dog, half-wolf

dispute: strive against

distance: hate

doubt: suspect

Doom: doomsday

dudgeon: handle

earnest: a token payment on account of the main sum due

ecstasy: madness, any strong emotion

expedition: haste

faculties: powers

fantastical: existing only in the fantasy, a creation of the imagination

farrow: litter

favour: face

fell: skin

file: list

fil'd: defield

flaw: gust of wind

fighty: fleet

forbid: accursed

foisons: abundance

franchis'd: free

furbish'd: newly made ready

gall: bitterness

get: beget

grac'd: full of grace

gulf: stomach

harness: armour

Harpier: a familiar spirit

Hecat: so spelt (and pronounced) in the Folio, one of the goddesses in the underworld

hie: hasten

house-keeper: watch-dog

hurly-burly: confusion

husbandry: confusion

Hyrcan: Caspian

incarnadine: make red

initiate: belonging to a novice

interdiction: exclusion

intermission: interval

intrenchant: that cannot be cut

invention: falsehood

jump: risk

jutty frieze: projection on a building

largess: gift of money

latch: catch

lated: belated

lighted: newly come to earth

lily-liver'd: cowardly

limited: allotted

line: aid

log'd: (of corn) laid flat

luxurious: vicious

magot-pies: magpies

mansionary: home

mated: confounded

maw: jaw

measure: quantity of drink, so 'toast'

metaphysical: supernatural

mettle: the same word as 'metal', hard substance, iron disposition

minion: darling

missives: messengers

moe: more

mortified: dead

nave: navel

nice: fastidious

nightgown: dressing-gown

nonpareil: without a parellel

oblivious: causing forget fulness

obscure bird: the owl

offices: (I) servants' quarters
(2) duties

old: slang for 'any amount of'

overcome: overshadow

owe: own

palpable: perceptible by the senses

patch: fool

pauser: that which restrains

peak: waste away

pent-house: a lean-to shed, so 'pent house' lid = eyelid

pester'd: troubled

physics pain: cures trouble

posset: hot drink, made of wine or ale and milk

posters: travelling post haste

power: army

present: immediate

pretence: plot, design

proof: armour

purveyor: fore-runner

quarry: heap of slain after a hunt

quell: murder

rapt: entranced

ravin: prey on

rawness: haste

register'd: recorded

remorse: pity

roof'd: under the roof, present

rooku: murky

round: dance

rugged: rough

scarf up: blindfold

seated: fixed

security: false sense of safety

self-abuse: self-deception

sensible: perceived by the senses

sere: dry

sewer: server

shaft: arrow

shard-borne: carried on its shiny wings

shough: shaggy-haired dog

sightless: invisile

skipping: nimble

skirr: scour

slab: thick, muddy

sleave: skein of silk

sleek: make smooth

sleights: tricks